THE
SECULARIZATION OF AMERICAN
EDUCATION

THE
SECULARIZATION OF AMERICAN EDUCATION

AS SHOWN BY STATE LEGISLATION, STATE CONSTITU-
TIONAL PROVISIONS AND STATE SUPREME
COURT DECISIONS

BY

SAMUEL WINDSOR BROWN, A.B., Ph.D.

NEW YORK / RUSSELL & RUSSELL

PRINTED IN THE UNITED STATES OF AMERICA

CONTENTS

THE
SECULARIZATION OF AMERICAN EDUCATION

INTRODUCTION

For somewhat over a century there has been going on in the United States a gradual but widespread elimination of religious and church influences from public education. During the early years of our history, especially during the colonial period, education and religion, the school and the church, were close allies. One of the aims of elementary education was to inculcate religious beliefs; of higher education, to prepare religious teachers. The subject matter of instruction was largely religious in its nature. Church authorities exercised considerable control over educational affairs. The warmest advocates of education were those who had in view the needs of the church. Today we find in every state a system of public education in which civic and industrial aims are dominant, in which religious instruction is either entirely eliminated or else reduced to the barest and most formal elements, and the control of which is vested well nigh exclusively in the state or some sub division thereof.

Two factors have been dominant in bringing about this transformation. The first of these is the conviction that a republic can securely rest only on an educated citizenship; the second is a sacred regard by the state for the religious opinion of the individual citizen.

So long as suffrage depended upon property, or some other qualification than mere manhood, the state needed to concern itself little about education. To private enterprise and religious zeal, assisted and encouraged at times by the state, could usually be intrusted the care of instructing the children and youth. But immediately manhood suffrage became universal, education began to assume too great an importance from the standpoint of

civic and national welfare for the state any longer to neglect it
or intrust it to any other than its own agents whom it could hold
responsible for standards and results.

So long as population regions were relatively homogeneous in
matters of religious faith nothing could be more natural than that
the public school should be used to transmit unto the children
the faith of the fathers.   For centuries, under an alliance of
church and state, more or less close, the schools had been so used.
But with the influx of immigration which set in about the third
decade of the last century and continued to grow with ever
increasing volume during the succeeding decades, composed
of the oppressed of all nations, our population regions, from being relatively homogeneous in religious matters, rapidly became
most heterogeneous.   The territories upon our western borders
rapidly filled with streams of settlers drawn from the original
sea-coast states as well as from various European countries.   Nor
were the original states unaffected by this influx of European
immigration.   All this resulted in a thorough mingling of diverse
religious and sectarian elements.

Education immediately began to assume great importance as
a means of Americanizing the diverse racial and cultural elements
composing our population, and the state began more and more to
foster schools and the means of instruction.   The great variety
of religious opinion and belief existing in every state or territory made the question of religious instruction in the schools
a crucial one.   On the one hand there was a widespread belief
that the chief purpose of all education was the formation of
character and that religion was a necessary element therein.   On
the other hand, there was a tenacious adherence by the representatives of every shade of religious belief, to the particular tenets
of their creed.   To allow their children to be taught less than they
believed, or other than they believed, was to them unthinkable.
So long as the determination of the instruction to be given and
the books to be used could be left to each individual community
a certain amount of adaptation was possible.   The majority at
least in each community could have its preferences therein carried
out.

But with state support and state control of education came, too,
centralization and uniformity, which were demanded by consid-

erations of efficiency and economy. Compulsory taxation for schools, compulsory attendance laws, and state or county courses of study, adoption of text-books, and certification of teachers, tended to minimize and to eliminate entirely the element of religion from the schools. As the units of administration widened from the lone community or district, where naturally there was the greatest degree of religious uniformity, to the state, made up of many communities, differing widely in their religious beliefs and practices, the majority vote became of less and less avail as a solution for our difficulties. Too many of our immigrant citizens had suffered from Old World intolerance to be willing to intrust to the state as a whole the determination of the nature of the religious instruction of their children. Rather than do this they were willing to forego religious instruction in the public schools altogether. Many of our native born citizens too and their fathers before them had suffered because of the union of the temporal and spiritual powers in the colonial governments. A majority must not be allowed to determine the religion of the minority. Of the two conflicting principles, freedom of religion, and majority rule, the more fundamental is that of religious freedom and it must prevail.

So it has come to pass that necessity has led the state to provide for education; and sectarian differences have made it necessary that this education should be non-sectarian or non-religious. The state has insisted upon the school just as it has insisted upon an army and a navy. And since a majority could not be appealed to to determine which religion, of the many prevalent among our people, should have a place in the public schools, it has been necessary to eliminate everything of a sectarian or religious nature. While the non-religious elements have no doubt frequently allied themselves with the movement toward secularization, yet it can hardly be said that they have been the controlling factor therein. Differences of religious belief and a sound regard on the part of the state for individual freedom in religious matters, coupled with the necessity for centralization and uniformity, rather than hostility toward religion as such, lie at the bottom of the movement toward the secular school.

I propose to show from our colonial school legislation, and occasional instances of state legislation, the prominent place occupied by religion in determining the aim and purpose of education during our early history, and the control exercised by the church thereover.   I propose to show from our state legislation and state constitutions how we have attempted to substitute for this education, dominated in large measure by the church, an education dominated by the state.   In addition I shall present some of the most important state supreme court decisions in which these laws and constitutional provisions, dealing with the subject of religious instruction and ecclesiastical control of education, have been interpreted by the courts.

CHAPTER I

THE RELIGIOUS AIM OF EDUCATION

That the aim of education in America as conceived at various times in our early history by our highest legislative authorities was largely religious, can be abundantly shown by citations from the enactments of the said authorities. Sometimes this purpose is set forth in the preamble to a law providing for the establishment of schools by some legislature; sometimes it is found in the royal instructions delivered to a governor; again it occurs in a charter granted to some school; still again we find it in a statement accompanying a grant of public money for some particular educational purpose. It shows itself in laws of a general educational nature, aiming at a common school education for all youth, as well as in provisions of a more limited scope looking to the education of the Indians, or to the preparation of ministers of the gospel.

Most of the enactments in which this religious purpose and aim is distinctly affirmed, or in which provision is made for religious instruction, bear dates prior to 1776. For this reason the date of the attainment of American nationality may well be taken as the dividing line between the dominance of the religious aim and that of the secular in educational affairs. It was six or eight decades later before the secular movement was in full swing, having gradually acquired momentum during the intervening period; but with 1776 the incorporation in our educational laws of distinct avowals of religious purpose or distinct provisions for religious instruction practically ceased. For this reason the few instances of the same which I have been able to find bearing dates subsequent to 1776 will be listed separately.

Connecticut: The legislation of Connecticut, from the middle of the seventeenth century till toward the close of the eighteenth, is especially clear as to this religious aim. The code of 1650 contains the following: " It is therefore ordered by this Court and

5

authority thereof, that the Select men of every Towne in the several precincts and quarters where they dwell, shall have a vigilant eye over their brethern and neighbors, to see, first, that none of them shall suffer so much barbarism in any of their families, as not to endeavor to teach by themselves or others, their children and apprentices so much learning as may enable them perfectly to read the English tongue, and knowledge of the capital laws . . .; also, that all masters of families, do, once a week, at least catechise their children and servants, in the grounds and principles of religion; and if any be unable to do so much, that then, at the least, they procure such children or apprentices to learn some short orthodox catechism, without book, that they may be able to answer to the questions that shall be propounded to them out of such catechism. . . ."

" It being one chief project of that old deluder, Satan, to keep men from the knowledge of the Scriptures, as in former times, keeping them in an unknown tongue, so in these latter times, by persuading them from the use of tongues, so that at least, the true sense and meaning of the original might be clouded with false glosses of saint seeming deceivers; and that learning may not be buried in the grave of our forefathers, in church and commonwealth, the Lord assisting our endeavors:" it is ordered by the authority of the Court that the means of education shall be provided for the children of the colonists. (Quoted from Hinsdale, American Educational History in Report of the Commissioner of Education, 1892-3, p. 1241-1242.) In the New Haven code of 1655 we find: " Whereas too many parents and masters, either through an over-tender respect to their own occasions and business, or not duly considering the good of their children and apprentices, have too much neglected duty in their education while they are young and capable of learning, it is ordered that the deputies for the particular court in each plantation within this jurisdiction for the time being, or where there are no such deputies, the constable or other officer or officers in public trust, shall from time to time have a vigilant eye over their brethren and neighbors within the limits of the said plantation, that all parents and masters do duly endeavor, either by their own ability and labor, or by improving such schoolmasters or other helps and means as the plantation doth afford, or the family may conveniently provide, that all their children and apprentices, as they grow capable, may, through God's blessing, attain at least so much as to be able duly to read the Scriptures and other good and profitable printed books in the English tongue, being their native language, and in some competent measure to understand the main grounds and principles of the Christian religion necessary to salvation. And to give a due answer to such plain and ordinary questions as may by the said deputies, officers or others, be propounded concerning the same. And when such deputies or officers, whether by information or examination, shall find any parent or master, one or more, negligent, he or they shall first give warning, and if thereupon due reformation follow, if the said parents or masters shall thenceforth seriously and constantly apply themselves to their duty in manner before expressed, the former neglect may be passed by; but if not, then the said deputies or other officer or officers, shall three months after such warning, present each such negligent person or persons to the next plantation court, where every such delinquent upon proof, shall be fined ten shillings to the plantation, to be levied as other fines. And if in any plantation there be no such court kept for the present, in such case the constable or other officer or officers warning such person or persons before the freemen, or so many of them as upon notice shall meet together, and proving the neglect after the warning, shall have power to levy the fines as aforesaid. But if, in three months after, there be no due care taken and continued for the education of such children or apprentices as aforesaid, the delinquent (without any further private warning) shall be proceeded against as before but the fine doubled. And lastly, if after the said warning, and fines paid or levied, the said deputies, officer or officers shall still find a continuance of the former negligence, if it be not obstinacy, so that such children or servants may be in danger to grow barbarous, rude and stubborn, through ignorance, they shall give due and reasonable notice, that every such parent or master be summoned to the next Court of Magistrates, who are to proceed as they find cause, either to a greater fine, taking security for due conformity to the scope and intent of this law, or may take such children and apprentices from such parents or masters, and place them for years, boys till they come to the age of one and twenty, and girls till they come to the age of eighteen years, with such others who shall better educate and govern them, both for public conveniency, and for the particular good of the said children or apprentices." (*New Haven Col. Rec.* 1653-1665, p. 583-84.)

In 1659 again we find the general court legislating in the interest of education for the avowed purpose of training men for the service of the church as well as the state. " The court looking upon it as their great duty to establish some course, that (through the blessing of God) learning may be promoted in the jurisdiction as a means for the fitting of instruments for public service in church and commonwealth, did order that £40 a year shall be paid by the treasurer for the furtherance of a grammar school for the use of the inhabitants of this jurisdiction, and that £8 more shall be disbursed by him for the procuring of books of Mr. Blinman such as shall be approved by Mr. Davenport and Mr. Pierson as suitable for this work. The appointing of the place where this school shall be settled, the person or persons to be employed, the time of beginning, etc., is referred to the Governor, Deputy Governor, the magistrates and ministers settled in the jurisdiction, or so many of them as upon due notice shall meet to consider of this matter." (*Records of the Colony or Jurisdiction of New Haven*, p. 301.)

In 1676 the general court recommended to the ministry to look into the state of religious instruction in families and urged the townsmen to assist the ministry for the reformation and education of the children, in good literature and the knowledge of the scriptures. (*Conn. Col. Rec.* 1665-1676, p. 281.) In 1680 the court urged the ministers to catechise young people under twenty in some orthodox catechism on the Sabbath days. (*Conn. Col. Rec.* 1678-1689, p. 65.)

In 1690 the court enacted the following: " . . . observing that notwithstanding the former orders made for the erudition of children and servants, there are many persons unable to read the English tongue and thereby uncapable to read the holy word of God, or the good laws of the colony, which evil, that it grow no farther upon their majesties subjects here, it is hereby ordered that all parents and masters shall cause their respective children and servants, as they are capable, to be taught to read distinctly the English tongue, and that the grand jurymen in each town do once in the year at least visit each family they suspect to neglect this order, and satisfy themselves whether all children under age and servants in such suspect families can read well the English tongue, or be in a good procedure to learn the same or not, and if they find any such children and servants not taught as their years are capable of, they shall return the names of the parents or masters of the said children so untaught, to the next county court, where the said parents or masters shall be fined twenty shillings for each child or servant whose teaching is or shall be neglected, contrary to this order, unless it shall appear to the satisfaction of the court, that the said neglect is not voluntary, but necessitated by the incapacity of the parent or masters or their neighbors, to cause them to be taught as aforesaid, or the incapacity of the said children to learn." (*Conn. Col. Rec.* 1689-1706, p. 30-31.)

An act of the legislature in 1714 " for the Encouragement and Better Improvement of Town Schools," makes it evident that the religious aim had an important place in the establishment and support of the public schools of the colony. " Forasmuch as the upholding and good ordering of the schools erected in towns by order of this Assembly, and partly maintained out of the public treasury, is of great importance to the public weal, and the neglect thereof will be the occasion of much ignorance, disorder, and profaneness. Be it therefore ordered and enacted by the Governor, Council, and representatives, in General Court Assembled, and by the authority of the same, that the civil authority, together with the selectmen in every town, or major part of them, shall inspect, and they are hereby empowered, as visitors, to inspect the state of all such schools as are appointed in the said town from time to time, and particularly once in each quarter of the year, at such times as they shall think proper to visit such schools, and inquire into the qualifications of the masters of such schools, and their diligence in attending to the service of the said schools, together with the proficiency of the children under their care. And they are hereby further required to give such directions as they shall find needful to render such schools most serviceable to the increase of that knowledge, civility and religion which is designed in the erecting of them. And it is further enacted, that if, in this inspection of the said schools, the said inspectors observe any such disorder, or misapplication of the public money allowed to the support of such schools, as render the said schools not so likely to attain the good ends proposed, they shall lay the same before the Assembly, that the proper orders in such cases necessary may be given." (*Conn. Col. Rec.* 1706-1716, p. 462.)

That this religious aim was the dominant one in the favorable attitude of the colony toward Yale College is clearly evident. The original act of incorporation of Yale is prefaced by the following: "Whereas several well-disposed and public spirited persons, of their sincere regard to and zeal for the upholding and propagating of the Christian protestant religion by a succession of learned and orthodox men, have expressed by petition their earnest desire that full liberty and privilege be granted unto certain undertakers, for the founding and suitably endowing and ordering a collegiate school, within this his Majesty's Colony of Connecticut, wherein youth may be instructed in the arts and sciences who, through the blessings of Almighty God, may be fitted for public employment both in church and civil state. To the intent therefore that all due encouragement be given to such pious resolutions and that so necessary and religious an undertaking may be set forward, supported, and well managed: Be it enacted by the Governor and Company of the said colony of Connecticut in general court assembled," etc. (*Conn. Col. Rec.* 1689-1706, p. 363.)

This religious aim is again set forward in an act of the Governor and council in 1703 granting to the trustees permission to raise money by brief throughout the colony for the maintenance of a tutor and the promotion of a college building: ". . . . furthermore the Governor and Council considering the very hopeful progress the reverend trustees have already made in the said affair, and the comfortable appearance that the said school under the present conduct of the said trustees will (through the divine blessing) conduce to the advancement of the interest of religion and general good of the colony, do therefore hereby recommend the aforesaid approved measure to all persons within the said colony, not doubting but that there will be in all a general readiness in their respective stations, and according to their respective circumstances to forward so good a work." (*Conn. Col. Rec.* 1689-1706, p. 454.)

In the preamble to an act passed in 1744, confirming and extending the powers of the trustees of Yale College, the general court expressed itself as follows: "And whereas, the said trustees, partners, and undertakers in pursuance to the aforesaid grant, liberty, and license, founded a collegiate school at New Haven, known by the name of Yale College, which has received the favorable benefactions of many liberal and piously disposed persons, and under the blessing of Almighty God has trained up many worthy persons for the service of God in the state as well as in the church," etc. (*Conn. Col. Rec.* IX, p. 113-118.)

In 1753 the legislature recommended the college unto the liberality of the people, and in doing so expressly avowed its religious aim: "Whereas one principal end proposed in erecting and supporting Yale College in New Haven was, to supply the churches of this colony with a learned, pious, and orthodox ministry, to which purpose it is requisite that the students of the said college should have the best instruction in divinity and the best patterns of preaching set before them; and whereas the settling a learned, pious, and orthodox professor of divinity in the said college would greatly tend to promote that good end and design: And whereas the present incomes of the said college are but in part sufficient to support such a professor: This assembly being desirous to promote and encourage such a good design, do hereby grant and allow of and order a general contribution to be made in all the religious societies in this colony, and recommend the same both to ministers and people, and order that the money raised thereby be remitted to the president of said college, to be improved by the corporation towards the support of such a professor." (*Conn. Col. Rec.* X, p. 213.)

From time to time the general court of Connecticut expressed in its legislation this religious aim as one of the motives for the education of the Indians. In 1723 Captain John Mason was urged "to set up a school among them and acquaint them in the Christian religion." (*Conn. Col. Rec.* 1717-1725, p. 429.) In 1727 the following law was enacted: "Whereas this Assembly is informed that many of the Indians in this government· put out their children to the English, to be brought up by them, and yet sundry of the persons having such children, do neglect to learn them to read and to instruct them in the principles of the Christian faith, so that such children are still in danger to continue heathens; which to prevent, Be it enacted by the Governor, Council and representatives, in General Court assembled, and by the authority of the same, that every person in this colony that hath taken or shall take any of the Indian children of this or the neighboring governments into the care of their families, are hereby ordered to use their utmost endeavor to teach them to read English, and also to instruct them in the principles of the Christian faith by catechising of them, together with other proper methods. And the selectmen and grand-jurors in the respective towns shall make diligent inquiry, whether the Indian children that are or may be put out as above, are by their masters or mistresses that have the care of them instructed and taught as abovesaid. And if upon inquiry the said officers shall find that any such master or mistress hath neglected their duty herein, after due warning given, then said officers, or any two of them, shall inform the next assistant or justice of the peace, upon which the said authority shall summon such master or mistress so informed against, to appear before them; and if upon examination it appear that said master or mistress hath neglected to instruct any Indian child or children put to them as aforesaid, they shall be fined at the discretion of said assistant or justice, not exceeding the sum of forty shillings, to be to the use of the school in the town where the master or mistress lives." (*Conn. Col. Rec.* VII, p. 102-103.)

In 1736 the following law regarding the education of the Indians was passed: "And to the end that so good a work may be furthered, be it enacted by the Governor, Council and Representatives, in General Court assembled, and by the authority of the same, that at the next public Thanksgiving that shall be appointed in this colony, there shall be a contribution attended in every ecclesiastical society or parish in this government, and that the money that shall be raised thereby shall be improved for the civilizing and Christianizing of the Indian natives in this colony (exclusive of the Moheags who are already provided for); and that his Honor, the Governor, send forth his order to the ministers of the respective parishes accordingly; and the Governor and Council, for the time being, are hereby appointed to receive the said contribution, and they are hereby directed carefully to improve the same for the end abovesaid; and they shall give an account of their doings therein to this Assembly, that no farther care from time to time may be taken. And whereas this Assembly are now informed that the said Nahantick Indians desire their children may be instructed, thereupon it is resolved that, the colony treasurer do pay out of the public treasury unto Messrs. Thomas Lee, of Lyme, and Stephen Prentiss, of New London, the sum of £15, who are appointed to receive the same, and therewith they shall hire some suitable person to instruct the said children to read, and also in the principles of the Christian religion, and also render an account to this Assembly of their disbursements of the money aforesaid." (*Conn. Col. Rec.* VIII, p. 37-38.)

The preamble to an act of the General Court in 1742, " Relating to, and for the better regulating schools of learning," is as follows: " Whereas, by sundry acts and laws of this assembly, they have founded, erected, endowed and provided for the maintenance of a college at New Haven, and inferior schools of learning in every town and parish, for the education and instruction of the youth of the colony, which have (by the blessing of God) been very serviceable to promote useful learning and Christian knowledge, and, more especially, to train up a learned and orthodox ministry for the supply of our churches;

" And inasmuch as the well ordering of such public schools is of great importance to the public weal, this Assembly by one Act entitled, An Act for the encouragement and better improvement of town schools, did order and provide, that the civil authority and selectmen in every town should be visitors to inspect the state of such schools, and to inquire into the qualification of the masters of them and the proficiency of the children, to give such directions as they shall think useful to render such schools most serviceable to increase that knowledge, civility and religion, which is destined in the erecting of them; and in case those visitors shall apprehend that any such schools are so ordered as not to be likely to attain to those good ends proposed, they shall lay the state thereof before the assembly, who shall give such orders thereupon as they shall think proper; as by the said act may more fully appear; And whereas the erecting of any other schools, which are not under the establishment and inspection aforesaid, may tend to train up youth in ill principles and practices, and introduce such disorders as may be of fatal consequence to the public peace and weal of this colony; which to prevent," etc. (*Conn. Col. Rec.* VIII, p. 500-501.)

In 1763 the following action was taken: The Assembly " seriously considering the present new and extraordinary prospect (by the blessing of Heaven on his Majesty's arms) doth greatly encourage an attempt to promote Christian knowledge and civility of manners among the Indian natives of this land, . . . grant and order a brief throughout this colony, recommending it to all inhabitants charitably and liberally to their ability to contribute to such pious and important purposes, and that the moneys so collected, be by the persons therewith intrusted, delivered to John Ledyard of Hartford, John Whiting of New Haven, David Gardiner of New London, David Rowland of Fairfield, Samuel Gray of Windham, and Elisha Sheldon of Litchfield, Esquires, each counties collections to their own respective receivers; which receivers are hereby directed to deliver the same to the treasurer of this colony . . ." "And it is further resolved, that said Mr. Wheelock do at his discretion as occasion may be, apply to Jonathan Trumble, Daniel Edwards, and George Wyllys, Esquires, for such moneys, parcel of such contributed sum as he shall apprehend to be necessary; which said committee, or any two of them, are hereby appointed, authorized and directed, to draw orders on said treasurer for such sum or sums thereof as shall be shown to them to be useful and necessary in the then present exigencies of said affair, until the whole is exhausted. Provided nevertheless, that if the state and circumstances of said undertaking by any means hereafter become so altered, as in the opinion of said last mentioned committee, to render the further prosecution or support of said affair impracticable or doubtful whether it may answer the good end and design, in such case they are hereby directed to desist drawing as aforesaid, and by the earliest opportunity to advise this Assembly thereof, to the end that such further order in the premises be taken as the present emergencies may recommend. Always provided such moneys be ultimately and wholly applied to the pious design of propagating the gospel among the heathen.

" And it is further ordered, that printed copies of this act be seasonably delivered to the several ministers of the gospel within this colony, who are hereby also directed to read this same in their respective congregations, and thereon appoint a time for making such collection." (*Conn. Col. Rec.* XII, p. 151-152.)

Delaware: The charter granted in 1640 by the Queen of Sweden for the settlement of a colony in Delaware set forth this religious aim of education in a provision that the patrons of the colony should be obliged to support at all times as many instructors and schoolmasters as the number of the inhabitants should seem to require; and to choose moreover, for this purpose, persons who had at heart the conversion of the pagan inhabitants to Christianity. (*Penn. Archives,* 2nd Series, p. 760, Harrisburg, 1877.)

Again in 1642 the following royal instructions were given to the governor: "Before all the Governor must labor and watch that he renders in all things to Almighty God, the true worship which is his due, the glory, the praise, and the homage which belong to him, and take good measures that the divine service is performed according to the true confession of Augsburg, the Council of Upsal, and the ceremonies of the Swedish Church, having care that all men, and especially the youth, be well instructed in all parts of Christianity, and that a good ecclesiastical discipline be observed and maintained." (*Penn. Archives,* 2nd Series, p. 773.)

Maryland: The "Petitionary Act for Free Schools," enacted by the legislature of Maryland in 1696, mentions the propagation of the gospel as one of the chief purposes of education: "II. And may it be enacted, by the King's most excellent majesty, by and with the advice, prayer and consent of this present General Assembly, and the authority of the same, that for the propagation of the Gospel, and the education of the youth of this province in good letters and manners, that a certain place or places, for a free school or schools or place of study of Latin, Greek, writing, and the like, consisting of one master, one usher, and one writing master or scribe, to a school, and one hundred scholars, more or less, according to the ability of the said free school, may be made, erected, founded, propagated and established under your royal patronage." (*Bacon's Laws* 1696, XVII.)

In a letter of the Maryland Assembly, directed to the Bishop of London in 1694, is set forth very definitely this religious aim of education: " May it please your lordship, under so glorious a reign, wherein by God's providence, his true religion has been so miraculously preserved, should we not endeavor to promote it, we should hardly deserve the name of good protestants or good subjects; especially considering how noble an example is set before us by their Majesties' royal foundation now vigorously carried on in Virginia. We have therefore in Assembly attempted to make learning an handmaid to devotion, and provided free schools in Maryland, to attend on their college in that country. We only beg their Majesties' confirmation of an act we have proposed for their establishment and of your lordship a share of that assistance and care you have taken in promoting so great and so good a design as that of the college. So charitable a founder of a school in opposition to that shop of poisoning principles set open in the Savoy, we are confident will favor our like pious designs in this province, wherein, instructing our youth in the orthodox, preserving them from the infection of heterodox tenets and fitting them for the service of church and state in this uncultivated part of the world, are our chiefest aim and end." (*Hist. Collection relating to the American Colonial Church,* Wm. S. Perry, IV, p. 1-2.)

" An Act for the Encouragement of Learning and Erecting Schools in the Several Counties within this Province," passed October 26, 1723, states this aim as follows: " Whereas the preceding Assemblies for some years past have had much at heart the absolute necessity they have lain under in regard both to duty and interest; to make the best provision in their power for the liberal and pious education of the youth of this province, and improving their natural abilities and acuteness (which seems not to be inferior to any), so as to be fitted for the discharge of their duties in the several stations and employments they may be called to, and employed in, either in regard to church or state," etc., all of which had succeeded so well, that this legislature (1723), for the same purposes, provided that there should be erected one school in each county of the province, and provided for the management and government of the same. (*Bacon's Laws* 1723, XIX.)

Massachusetts: The general court of Massachusetts in 1641 recommended that the elders make out a catechism for the instruction of youth in the grounds of religion. (*Mass. Col. Rec.* I, p. 328.) By the law of 1642 the chosen men of each town in Massachusetts were empowered to, " take account from time to time of all parents and masters and of their children concerning their calling and employment of their children, especially of their ability to read and understand the principles of religion and the capital laws of this country, and to impose fines upon such as shall refuse to render such accounts to them when they shall be required," etc. (*Mass. Col. Rec.* II, p. 8-9.)

In 1642 again an act of the General Court ordered that those having control of the college at Cambridge should " have from time to time full powers and authority to make and establish all such orders, statutes, and constitutions as they shall see necessary for the instituting, guiding, and furthering of the said college and the several members thereof from time to time in piety, morality and learning," etc. (*Mass. Col. Rec.* II, p. 30.) In 1652 the court requested voluntary contributions from the colonists for the assistance of Harvard College, on the grounds of the necessity of education for the purposes of the commonwealth and of the church. (*Mass. Col. Rec.* IV, Part I, p. 100-101.) In 1654 because of its benefit to church and state the court made an appropriation of £100 to Harvard besides renewing the grant of the profit of a ferry formerly granted unto the college. (*Mass. Col. Rec.* IV, Part I, p. 205.)

The law of 1647 ordering, " that every township in this jurisdiction, after the Lord hath increased them to the number of fifty householders, shall then appoint one within their town to teach all such children as shall resort to him to write and read " was avowedly, in part, prompted by religious considerations. (*Mass. Col. Rec.* II, p. 203.) The law of 1712, "An Act against intemperance, immorality and profaneness, and for reformation of manners," dealing in part with education, provides that none shall teach " but such as are of sober and good conversation and have the allowance and approbation of the selectmen of the town," on the grounds that " the well educating and instructing of children and youth in families and schools are a necessary means to propagate religion and good manners." The preamble to an act of 1768 — An act in further addition to the several acts for the settlement and support of schools and school masters — runs as follows: "Whereas, it may happen that where towns or districts consist of several precincts, some such precincts may be disposed to expend more for the instruction of children and youth, in useful learning, within their own bounds, than, as parts of such towns or districts, they are, by law, held to do, and no provision has hitherto been made to enable precincts to raise money for that purpose; and whereas the encouragement of learning tends to the promotion of religion and good morals, and the establishment of liberty, civil and religious;" etc. (*Acts and Resolves* IV, p. 988.)

New Hampshire: In 1769 George III granted a charter to Dartmouth College in New Hampshire, one of the purposes of which institution as expressed in this charter was, "to promote learning among the English, and be a means to supply a great number of churches and congregations which are likely soon to be formed in that new country, with a learned and orthodox ministry . . ." For this purpose it provides that the trustees thereof shall, "elect, nominate, and appoint a professor in divinity, who shall and may read lectures in theology, instruct the students in the science of divine truths and the knowledge of the Holy Scriptures, who also may be president of the college, or not, as the trustees shall see meet and convenient." A second purpose is set forth in the words, "considering the premises and being willing to encourage the laudable design of spreading Christian knowledge among the savages of our American wilderness," etc. (Quoted by Smith in *History of Dartmouth College,* p. 457-464.)

New Jersey: In the royal instructions to Governor Bernard of New Jersey in 1758 the religious aim of education is clearly shown. "Sec. 67. And it is our further will and pleasure that you recommend to the assembly to enter upon proper methods for the erecting and maintaining of schools in order to the training up of youth to reading and to a necessary knowledge of the principles of religion." (*New Jersey Archives,* 1st Series, Part IX, p. 68-69.) The charter granted to Queens College, New Jersey, by George III in 1770 states that it is intended, "to provide learning for the benefit of the community and advancement of the Protestant religion of all denominations; and more especially to remove as much as possible the necessity our said loving subjects have hitherto been under, of sending their youth intended for the ministry, to a foreign country for education, and of being subordinate to a foreign ecclesiastical jurisdiction." (*The Charter of Queens College in New Jersey*, with Appendix, printed for the Trustees at New Brunswick, quoted by Clews, p. 336.)

New Netherlands: In 1664 the Director-General and Council of New Netherlands enacted the following ordinance: "Ordinance of the Director-General and Council of New Netherlands, for the better and more careful instruction of youth in the principles of the Christian religion. Whereas it is highly necessary and most important that the youth from childhood up be instructed not only in reading, writing, and arithmetic, but especially and chiefly in the principles and fundamentals of the reformed religion, according to the lesson of that wise king Solomon,— train up a child in the way he shall go, and when he is old he will not depart from it,— so that in time such men may proceed therefrom, as may be fit to serve their Fatherland as well in the church as in the state. This then being taken into particular consideration by the Director-General and Council of New Netherlands, because the number of children is, merciful blessing of the Lord, considerably increasing here, they have deemed it necessary, in order that so useful and God-acceptable a work may be the more effectually promoted, to recommend and command the schoolmasters, as we do hereby, that they shall appear in the church, with the children committed to their care and intrusted to them, on Wednesday, before the commencement of the sermon, in order, after the conclusion of Divine Service, that each may in the presence of the reverend ministers and the elders who may be present, examine his scholars as to what they have committed to memory of the Christian commandments and catechism, and what progress they have made; after which performance, the children shall be dismissed for that day, and allowed a decent recreation." (*Laws and Ordinances of New Netherlands*, p. 461.) Among the laws confirmed by the delegates to a convention at Hempstead, Long Island, in 1665, was a provision which shows the religious aim of education: "The constable and overseers are strictly required frequently to admonish the inhabitants of instructing their children and servants in matters of religion and the laws of the country." (*Col. Laws of New York,* I, p. 26.)

New York: The charter granted by George II to the College of the Province of New York in 1755 contained the following provision: "Know ye that of our especial grace, certain knowledge, and mere motion, we have willed, granted, constituted, and appointed, and by these presents, do will and grant to the Governors of the College of the Province of New York, in the city of New York, in America, and to their successors, that from time to time, and at all times hereafter forever, there may, and shall be in the said college, a professor of Divinity of the Reformed Protestant Dutch Church, for the instruction of such youth as may intend to devote themselves to the sacred ministry in those churches, in this our province of New York, that are in communion with, and conform to the doctrine, discipline, and worship established in the United Provinces, by the National Synod of Dort; and any other students that may be desirous to attend his lectures." The selection of such professor of divinity was left to the judgment of the ministers, elders, and deacons of the Reformed Protestant Dutch Church in the City of New York, with the single condition that he should always be a member of and in communion with the said Reformed Protestant Dutch Church. (*Charters, Acts, and Official Documents Relating to Columbia University,* compiled by John B. Pine, New York, 1895, p. 26-28.)

North Carolina: In 1766 the legislature of North Carolina in the preamble to an act incorporating a society for promoting and establishing a public school at Newbern and making it a grant of public funds states the religious purpose of the school as follows: "Whereas a number of well disposed persons, taking into consideration the great necessity of having a proper school or public seminary of learning established, whereby the rising generation may be brought up and instructed in the principles of the Christian religion, and fitted for the offices and several purposes of life, have at a great expense erected and built, in the town of Newbern, a convenient house for the purposes aforesaid; and being desirous that the same may be established by law on a permanent footing, so as to answer the good purposes by the said persons intended;" etc. (*Revisal* 1773, p. 359-361.)

Pennsylvania: The religious aim of education is shown in a law passed in Pennsylvania in 1683, part of which reads as follows: "all persons in this province and territories thereof, having children, and all the guardians or trustees of orphans, shall cause such to be instructed in reading and writing; so that they may be able to read the scriptures;" etc. (*Charters and Laws of the Province of Pennsylvania,* p. 142.) The Friends Free School received from the proprietary government of Pennsylvania in 1711 a charter which declares in a portion of the preamble the religious purpose of public schools. " Whereas the prosperity and welfare of any people depend, in a great measure, upon the good education of youth, and their early instruction in the principles of true religion and virtue, and qualifying them to serve their country and themselves, by breeding them in reading, writing, and learning of languages, and useful arts and sciences suitable to their sex, age, and degree; which cannot be effected in any manner so well as by erecting public schools for the purposes aforesaid." (Quoted by Wickersham, p. 44-48.) The charter granted in 1753 to the Academy and Charitable School in the Province of Pennsylvania by the proprietary government states in its preamble, the religious aim of education. " Whereas the well-being of a society depends on the education of their youth, as well as, in great measure, the eternal welfare of every individual, by impressing on their tender minds principles of morality and religion, instructing them in the several duties they owe to society in which they live, and one towards another, giving them the knowledge of languages, and other parts of useful learning necessary thereto, in order to render them serviceable in the several public stations to which they may be called."[1]

Rhode Island: The act of 1764 incorporating the University of Rhode Island and Providence Plantation provided that " sectarian differences of opinion shall not make any part of the public and classical instruction; although all religious controversies may be studied freely, examined and explained by the president, pro-

[1] Quoted in Circular of Information, No. 2, 1892, issued by the U. S. Bureau of Education, entitled, Benjamin Franklin and the University of Pennsylvania, p. 68.

fessors, and tutors in a personal, separate, and distinct manner, to the youth of any or each denomination; and above all, a constant regard to be paid to, and effectual care taken of, the morals of the college." (*Records of the Colony of Rhode Island and Provincial Plantations in New England,* VI, p. 385-391.)

South Carolina: In 1710 the legislature of South Carolina passed "An Act for the Founding and Erecting of a Free School for the Use of the Inhabitants of South Carolina," which began as follows: "Whereas it is necessary that a free school be erected for the instruction of the youth of this province in grammar and other arts and sciences and useful learning, and also in the principles of the Christian religion;" etc. (*Statutes at Large of South Carolina,* T. Cooper, 1837, II, p. 342-346.)

In 1712 there was passed by the proprietary government an act establishing a free school in Charleston, in which the schoolmaster should be capable to catechise and instruct the youth in the principles of the Christian religion. (*Statutes at Large of South Carolina,* II, p. 389-396.) An act of 1734 for establishing a free school at the town of Dorchester, in the parish of St. George, Berkeley County, likewise contained a provision that the master should be capable, "to catechise and instruct the youth in the principles of the Christian religion." (*Statutes at Large of South Carolina,* III, p. 378-383.)

Virginia: In 1618 the following instructions were given by the Council of the Virginia Company to the Colonial Governor of Virginia: "Whereas by a special grant and license from his Majesty a general contribution over this realm hath been made for the building and planting of a college for the training up of the children of those infidels in the true religion, moral virtue, and civility, and for other godliness, we do, therefore, according to a former grant and order, hereby ratify, confirm and ordain that a convenient place be chosen and set out for the planting of a university at the said Henrico in the time to come, and that in the meantime preparation be there made for the building of the said college for the children of the infidels according to such instructions as we shall deliver. And we will and ordain that ten thousand acres, partly of the lands they impaled and partly of the lands within the territory of the said Henrico, be allotted and set out for the endowing of the said university and college with convenient possessions."[1]

The Grand Assembly in 1660-1661 enacted the following: "Whereas the want of able and faithful ministers in this country deprives us of these great blessings and mercies that always attend upon the service of God, which want, by reason of our great distance from our native country, cannot in probability be always supplied from thence, Be it enacted, that for the advance of learning, education of youth, supply of the ministry, and promotion of piety, there be land taken upon purchases for a college and free school, and that there be with as much speed as may be convenient, housing erected thereon for entertaining of students and scholars." (*Hening* II, p. 25.) At the same session it was ordered that the several county courts subscribe such sums as they might see fit and take the subscriptions of such persons as should see fit to subscribe for the establishment and maintenance of a college of students of the liberal arts and sciences, "for the advancement of learning, promoting piety, and provision of an able and successive ministry in this country." (*Hening* II, p. 37.) The charter granted by William and Mary in 1692 to the College of William and Mary declared: "Forasmuch as our well-beloved and faithful subjects, constituting the General Assembly of our Colony of Virginia, have had it in their minds, and have proposed to themselves, to the end that the Church of Virginia may be furnished with a seminary of ministers of the gospel, and that the youth may be piously educated in good letters and manners, and that the Christian faith may be propagated among the Western Indians, to the glory of Almighty God; to make, found, and establish a certain place of universal study, or perpetual College of Divinity, Philosophy, Languages, and other good arts and sciences;" . . . "We taking the premises seriously into our consideration, and earnestly desiring, that as far as in us lies, true philosophy, and other good and liberal arts and sciences may be promoted, and that the orthodox Christian faith may be propagated;" etc. (*History of the College of William and Mary from its Foundation,* 1660 to 1874.)

---

[1] Quoted by Neill, History of the Virginia Company, p. 137, from manuscript instructions to Yeardley, *Virginia Records,* small folio in Library of Congress.

I have been able to discover the following laws in which the religious aim is incorporated bearing dates subsequent to 1776.

Connecticut: An act of the Connecticut legislature entitled, "An Act for the Educating and Governing of Children," contains the following: "All parents and masters of children, shall by themselves or others teach and instruct, or cause to be taught and instructed all such children as are under their care and government, according to their ability, to read the English tongue well and to know the laws against capital offenses; And if unable to do so much, then at best to learn some short orthodox catechism without book, so as to be able to answer to the questions that shall be propounded to them out of such catechism, by their parents, masters or ministers when they shall call them to an account of what they have of that kind." (*Laws* 1796, Hudson and Goodwin printers, p. 60.)

Georgia: The preamble to an act of the legislature of Georgia, incorporating Oglethorpe University, passed in 1835, reads as follows: " Whereas, the cultivation of piety and the diffusion of useful knowledge greatly tend to preserve the liberty and to advance the prosperity of a free people, and whereas these important objects are best obtained by training the minds of the rising generation in the study of useful science, and imbuing their hearts with the sentiments of religion and virtue; and whereas it is the duty of an enlightened and patriotic legislature to authorize, protect and foster institutions established for the promotion of these important objects;" etc. (*Act* Dec. 21, 1835.) The same views were repeated in the Act of December 24th, 1836, incorporating the Southern Baptist College.

Illinois: The Illinois legislature in 1836 incorporated the Chatham Manual Labor School providing that each and every denomination of Christians might establish in connection therewith a professorship in theology for the promulgation of their peculiar religious tenents, they severally furnishing the funds for the support of the same. (*Act* Jan. 9, 1836.)

Maine: In 1821 the legislature of Maine made it the duty of the presidents, professors and tutors of colleges, and the preceptors of academies, and all other instructors of youth, to take diligent care and exert their best endeavors to impress on the minds of children and youth committed to their care and instruction, the principles of piety and justice, and a sacred regard to truth, love to their country, humanity, and universal benevolence. (*Act* March 15, 1821.) The Revised Statutes of 1903 provide for the teaching of the fundamental truths of Christianity in the state normal schools. (*Revised Statutes* 1903, Ch. 15, Sec. 109.)

New York: The Act of 1784 establishing the University of New York contains the following: " Whenever any religious body or society of men shall deem it proper to institute a professorship in the said university for the promotion of their religious tenents, or for any other purpose not inconsistent with religion, morality, and the laws of the state, and shall appropriate a sum for that purpose, not being less than 200 bushels of wheat per annum, the regents shall cause the same to be applied as the donors shall direct." (*Session Laws* 1784, Ch. 51, Act May 1, 1784.)

South Carolina: The Revised Statutes of 1873 of South Carolina provided that one of the departments of the University of South Carolina should be a school of mental and moral philosophy, sacred literature, and evidences of Christianity. (*Revised Statutes* 1873, Ch. XLII, Sec. 13, Par. 5.)

CHAPTER II

THE RELIGIOUS INSTRUCTION OF ORPHANS AND THE INMATES OF INDUSTRIAL SCHOOLS, REFORM SCHOOLS, AND PENAL INSTITUTIONS

The problem facing the state in the education of these special classes is radically different from that in the education of ordinary children and youth. When religion is excluded from the course of study of our public schools and colleges it is common to justify the exclusion in part on the ground that the home and the church rather than the state should provide for religious instruction. But in the case of orphans and the inmates of industrial schools, reform schools, and penal institutions, the parents having been removed by death, or the children and youth having been taken out of the control of the parents, the state must assume full responsibility for their moral and religious training. If the state fails or refuses to provide it, or to allow others to provide it, then these classes are excluded, absolutely, from all benefit of such instruction.

The problem is further intensified by the fact that the inmates of the institutions above named, and frequently the orphans also, make up morally the weakest element of our population. The refusal or inability of the state to impart religious instruction unto them brings about the curious phenomenon of trying to prepare for citizenship, an element of society in the education of which, the religious element, if it has any value anywhere, must be of supreme worth, without any employment of the same.

The wording of our laws shows that the state has realized the responsibility resting upon it, and while, as I shall show later, religious instruction has been very generally entirely eliminated from the education of normal children, in dealing with the delinquent classes the state has not failed to make use of religion as an instrument and help in moral instruction. Incidentally, this fact substantiates one of the things for which I am contending, namely, that it is not hostility to religion on the part of the state

26

which has prompted it to exclude religion from the schools, but rather sectarian differences, coupled with the feeling that, normally, the home and the church can more adequately provide for religious instruction than can the public school.

The few cases of legislation which I cite, dealing with the religious education of orphans, all bear dates within the colonial period, and reveal a concern on the part of the state not only for moral and religious instruction, but often for sectarian religious instruction as well, seeing to it that the children are educated in the particular religious tenets of their deceased parents. While most of the laws already cited, in which the religious aim of education is set forth, belong to the colonial period, those having to do with the education of the morally delinquent, since the institutions provided for the care of the same are of relatively recent date, have been enacted since the middle of the nineteenth century and frequently are the laws in force at the present time.

In these laws, provision is made for religious instruction and for holding religious services for the benefit of the inmates of the institutions in question, and there frequently is discernible the same care that children shall be instructed in the religious tenets of their parents, as is shown in the laws cited dealing with the care of orphans during the colonial period. Care is taken that representatives of all religious denominations shall be accorded equal privileges in the imparting of religious instruction and the holding of religious services therein, and that no sectarian views shall dominate the same. Only rarely do we find religious instruction as such forbidden in these institutions. The control of all such institutions, however, which receive state aid must be exclusively in the hands of the state.

During colonial days it was a common practice to bind out or apprentice orphan children, so that frequently, no doubt, the laws containing the expression, " masters of apprentices," or " guardians of children," occurring in Chapter I, have to do with the education of orphans. In a few instances, however, laws passed during the colonial period make direct reference to the religious education of this class of children.

Maryland: The colony of Maryland enacted in 1671 that " care must be taken to have the children educated in the religion of the deceased parents." (*Maryland Archives, Proceedings and Acts* 1666-1676, p. 325.) In 1715 a most stringent law was passed strongly favoring the Protestant faith, " provided always that where any person, being a Protestant, shall die, and leave a widow and children, and such widow shall intermarry any person of the Romish communion, or be herself of that opinion and profession, it shall and may be lawful for his Majesty's Governor and Council, within this province, upon application to them made, to remove such child or children out of the custody of such parents, and place them where they may be securely educated in the Protestant religion." (*Bacon's Laws* 1715, Ch. XXXIX.)

North Carolina: A law of North Carolina in the early eighteenth century provided, " that all orphans shall be educated and provided for according to their rank and degree, out of the income or interest of their estates or stocks, if the same shall be sufficient; otherwise such orphan shall be bound apprentice to some handicraft trade, (the master or mistress of such orphans not being of the profession of the people called Quakers) until they shall come of age." (*A Collection of All the Public Acts of the Assembly of the Province of North Carolina,* Newbern 1752, p. 30.)

Pennsylvania: A Pennsylvania law passed in 1683 reads in part as follows: "All persons in this province and territories thereof, having children, and all the guardians or trustees of orphans, shall cause such to be instructed in reading and writing; so that they may be able to read the scriptures;" etc. (*Charters and Laws of the Province of Pennsylvania,* p. 142.)

Virginia: A law of the Virginia legislature of 1643 provided that all overseers and guardians of orphans should " educate and instruct them according to their best endeavors in Christian religion and in rudiments of learning." (*Hening* I, p. 260-261.)

The following laws provide for religious instruction or religious services in industrial schools, reform schools or penal institutions.

Colorado: With regard to its Parental or Truant Schools the state of Colorado has enacted the following: " No religious instruction shall be given in such schools except such as is allowed by law to be given in public schools; but the board of education shall make suitable regulations so that the inmates may receive religious training in accordance with the belief of the parents of such children, either by allowing religious services to be held in the institution or by arranging for attendance at public service elsewhere." (*Acts* 1901, p. 365, Par. 4, *Mills Annotated Statutes*, Rev. Sup. 1891-1905, Sec. 4015 K.)

Connecticut: Connecticut has enacted the following: " Equal privileges shall be granted to clergymen of all religious denominations to impart religious instruction to the inmates of the Connecticut School for Boys, and the Connecticut Industrial School for Girls; and every reasonable opportunity shall be allowed such clergymen to give such inmates, belonging to their respective denominations, religious and moral instruction; and the teachers of each of said institutions shall prescribe reasonable times and places, not inconsistent with its proper management, when and where such instruction may be given, which shall be open to all who choose to attend." (*Code* 1902, Sec. 2847.)

Georgia: In Georgia we find the following law with regard to the powers and duties of the principal of the Academy for the Deaf and Dumb: " He shall be the sole official medium of communication between the board and the subordinate officers and employees of the institution and shall have the exclusive direction and control of the system of religious and moral instruction." (*Code* 1895, Sec. 1322.) By Section 1320 the principal is made responsible to the trustees and his acts made subject to their veto.

Idaho: In Idaho the following is the law with regard to the Industrial Training School: " The superintendent shall provide for the holding of religious services on the Sabbath day for the inmates of said school but no sectarian views shall control the services." (*School Laws* 1905, p. 21, Sec. 13.)

Illinois: The law of Illinois respecting Parental or Truant Schools is as follows: " No religious instruction shall be given in such school except such as is allowed by law to be given in public schools; but the Board of Education shall make suitable regulation so that the inmates may receive religious training in accordance with the belief of the parents of said children, either by allowing religious services to be held in the institution or by arranging for attendance at public service elsewhere." (*Act* April 24, 1899, Sec. 4, *Revised Statutes* 1906, Sec. 436.) With regard to Industrial Schools for Girls the following is found: "All industrial schools for girls in this state shall be subject to the same visitation, inspection and supervision of the Board of State Commissioners of Public Charities as the charitable and penal institutions of the state, and avoiding as far as practicable, sectarianism, suitable provision shall be made for the moral and religious instruction of the inmates of all industrial schools for girls in this state." (*Revised Statutes* 1906, Ch. 122, Sec. 333.)

Massachusetts: In an act of the Massachusetts legislature incorporating the Boston Farm School is the following: " All boys so taken and admitted into the school, shall be maintained, employed and educated therein, and shall be instructed in their moral and religious duties and in the knowledge usually communicated in the common town schools." (*Session Laws* 1833, Ch. CXXXV, *Act* March 19, 1833.)

Minnesota: In 1870 the legislature of Minnesota enacted the following with regard to the Minnesota State Reform School: " The board of managers shall establish such regulations respecting religious and moral education, training, employment, discipline, and safe keeping of its inhabitants as may be deemed expedient and proper.

" All persons committed to the Minnesota State Reform School shall be allowed, in all cases of sickness, spiritual advice and spiritual ministrations from any recognized clergyman of the denomination or church to which said inmates may respectively belong; such advice and ministration to be given within sight of the person or persons having charge of such inmates; but if the sick person or persons seeking it, desire religious consolation out of hearing of any officer of said institution, they in such case, shall not be debarred the right by any rule of such school." (*Act* March 3, 1870, Sec. 3 and 8.) By a subsequent act this privilege of spiritual advice and consolation was extended to all inmates and made much more specific, and it was made much more mandatory that the school authorities allow it. "All persons committed to any prison or reform school or other place of confinement in said state shall be allowed spiritual advice and spiritual ministration from any recognized clergyman of the denomination or church to which said persons so committed or received may respectively belong, and have belonged prior to their being so committed or received into such state prison or reform school or other place of confinement; such advice or ministration to be given within the prison or reform school or other building where the inmates thereof are required by law to be confined or imprisoned, in such manner as will secure to such persons the free exercise of their religious belief, and such religious consolation, advice and ministration shall be allowed separate and apart and out of the presence and hearing of any person other than the clergyman who is ministering to such inmates.

" It shall be the duty of the Board of Managers or persons or officers having control and management of said institution to set apart not less than one hour (and more if necessary) on the first day of each week in which any clergyman in good standing of any church or denomination may freely minister to and impart moral and religious instruction to those of the said inmates or children who respectively belong thereto or have belonged thereto prior to their being so committed or received therein; and to afford and grant to such clergymen such reasonable and proper facilities as may be necessary to enable them to freely and properly discharge their duties as ministers and spiritual advisers to the said inmates, and to provide and furnish to such clergymen on such occasions a room or apartment where they may be enabled to freely and properly discharge their duties as such clergymen." (*Act* March 5, 1874, *General Statutes* 1894, Sec. 3633-3634.)

Montana: The Montana law with regard to the Industrial School reads as follows: " No religious instruction shall be given in said school except such as is allowed by law to be given in public schools; but the board of trustees may make suitable regulations so that the inmates may receive religious training in accordance with the belief of the parents of such children, by arranging for attendance at public services elsewhere." (*School Laws* 1903, p. 90, Sec. 1925.)

New Jersey: By an act of the New Jersey legislature in 1831 religious and well-inclined persons of any Christian denomination were to be admitted to the state prison on Sundays to perform divine service. (*Act* Jan. 25, 1831.) By an act of 1860 in the same state a moral instructor at the state prison was provided for at an annual salary of $600. (*Act* March 22, 1860. *Session Laws* 1860, Ch. CCX.)

CHAPTER III

THE ECCLESIASTICAL CONTROL OF EDUCATION

Laws granting the church or its representatives more or less control over education are a natural corollary of laws in which religion is recognized as a major aim of education.

The church is the special repository of religion. Her ministers are assumed to be religious experts. Hence who could be better qualified to set standards and determine proficiency in religious education than the minister? If the school exists for inculcating the religion of a particular church, why should there not be a religious test to assure the orthodoxy of the teacher? And especially when the school exists for training the ministry of a particular church, who could be better qualified to control the teaching of the school than the representative of the church?

Moreover, the ministry have ever been as a rule a relatively highly educated class. Before the development of a special set of officials for supervising education what more natural than that the state should make use of these learned men, eminently qualified, and having sufficient leisure, to perform the supervisory function? In a society where the church and state are intimately related, what more natural than that the church and its machinery, organized specifically for imparting religious instruction, should be depended on by the state to control education when the state had as yet evolved no other special agency of control?

As with the laws favoring the religious aim of education, the laws recognizing or authorizing ecclesiastical control in education were most numerous during the colonial period. They were enacted in at least nine of the original thirteen colonies, but in only half a dozen or so of the state governments out of a total of forty-eight have they ever been in force. Such laws belonging to the colonial period may be summed up under three heads: (1) The Examination, Certification, or Appointment of Teachers by Some Church Authority. (2) The Establishment of Religious

33

Tests for Educational Officers. (3) The Delegation of Supervisory, Administrative, or Teaching Powers to Church Authorities. The few instances of such legislation of dates later than 1776 will be listed separately.

1. The Examination, Certification, or Appointment of Teachers by Some Church Authority

Massachusetts: In 1701 the legislature of Massachusetts enacted that every grammar school master should be approved by the minister of the town, and the ministers of the two next adjacent towns or by any two of them. (*Acts and Resolves* 1, p. 470.)

New Jersey: In 1758 the following instructions from the Crown were received by the royal governor of New Jersey: " We do further direct that no schoolmaster be henceforth permitted to come from England to keep school in the said province without the license of the said bishop of London," etc. (*New Jersey Archives* 1st Series, IX, p. 68-69.)

New York: In 1663 the provincial government agreed to pay twenty-five florins heavy money in support of a teacher in the village of Bushwyck on condition that he be examined by the ministers of the city and found competent. (*Albany Records* XX, p. 297.)[1] The royal governor in 1686 received the following instructions: "And we do further direct that no schoolmaster be henceforth permitted to come from England and to keep school within our province of New York without the license of the said Archbishop of Canterbury." (*New York Colonial Documents,* III, p. 372.) In royal instructions of January 1, 1689 (*New York Colonial Documents,* III, p. 688), March 7, 1692 (*New York Colonial Documents,* III, p. 821), August 31, 1697 (*New York Colonial Documents,* IV, p. 288), and December 27, 1709 (*New York Colonial Documents,* V, p. 135), the license was required to be had from the Bishop of London instead of from the Archbishop of Canterbury. The charter granted by William III in 1696 to the Reformed Dutch Church contains the following: "And our will and pleasure further is, and we do hereby declare that the

[1] Quoted by Clews, p. 218.

ministers of said church, for the time being, shall and
may, by and with the consent of the elders and deacons
of the said church, for the time being, nominate and appoint a schoolmaster and such other under-officers as they
shall stand in need of." (*Ecclesiastical Records of the State of
New York*, Vol. II, p. 1136-1165.) In 1755 George II, in granting a charter for the establishment of a professorship of divinity
in the College of the Province of New York, provided as follows: "And we do, by these presents, will, give, grant, and
appoint, that such professor shall be from time to time, and at
all times hereafter, nominated, chosen, and appointed by the
ministers, elders, and deacons of the Reformed Protestant Dutch
Church in the City of New York, for the time being, when they
shall see fit to make such nomination, choice, and appointment.
And they are hereby empowered and authorized to make such
nomination, choice, and appointment; and they are hereby required to certify such nomination, choice and appointment, to
the governors of the said college, under their corporation seal."
(*Charters, Acts and Official Documents Relating to Columbia
University* compiled by John B. Pine, New York, 1895, p. 26-
28.)

Virginia: In an act for incorporating the Borough of Nor-
folk in 1752, the legislature of Virginia, after providing for a
schoolmaster, specified as follows: " Which said master, before
he be received or admitted to keep school, shall undergo an
examination before the masters of the College of William and
Mary, and minister of Elizabeth parish, for the time being, and
produce a certificate of his capacity, and also a license from the
Governor, or commander-in-chief of this dominion, for the time
being." (*Hening* VI, p. 265.) An act passed in 1756 providing, among other things, for founding a free school in each of
the parishes of Abingdon and Ware, and empowering trustees
and governors to appoint schoolmasters specified as follows:
" Which masters, before they be admitted to keep school, shall
undergo an examination before the minister of the parish in
which the school he shall be appointed master of shall be situated,
and produce a certificate of his capacity, and also a license from
the governor or commander-in-chief of the dominion, for the

time being," etc. (*Hening* VII, p. 41-43.) In 1759 an act for better regulating Eaton's Charity School, empowered the trustees and governors of the school, " to nominate and appoint when, and as often as they shall think good, such person as they shall approve of to be master of the said charity school, such master having been first examined by the minister of the said parish for the time being, and producing from him a certificate of his capacity, and a license from the governor or commander-in-chief of this dominion, for the time being," etc. (*Hening* VII, p. 317-320.)

2. The Establishment of Religious Tests for Educational Officers

Laws requiring teachers and members of boards of control to be of some particular religious faith were a common feature of colonial school legislation. They must hold such faith in order to be eligible to appointment and sometimes provision was made that in case of a change in their religious views they should forfeit their office.

Maryland: An act of the legislature of Maryland, passed in 1723, provided for the distribution of public funds to schools in which the teachers were to be members of the Church of England, " and the visitors aforesaid are likewise hereby directed to take all proper methods for the encouraging good schoolmasters, that shall be members of the Church of England, and of a pious and exemplary lives and conversations, and capable of teaching well the grammar, good writing, and the mathematics, if such can conveniently be got." (*Bacon's Laws* 1723, Ch. XIX.)

Massachusetts: The following measure was passed by the General Court of Massachusetts May 31, 1654: " Forasmuch as it greatly concerns the welfare of this country that the youth thereof be educated, not only in good literature, but sound doctrine, this court doth therefore commend it to the serious consideration and special care of the overseers of the college and the selectmen in the towns, not to admit or suffer any such to be continued in the office or place of teaching, educating, or instructing of youth or children in the college or schools that have manifested themselves unsound in the faith or scandalous in their lives, and not giving due satisfaction according to the rules of Christ." (*Colonial Records* IV, Pt. I, p. 182-183.)

New Jersey: In 1770 George III granted a charter for the establishment of Queens College in New Jersey in which appears the following provision for a religious test to be observed in the selection of a president: "And also, we do hereby for us, our heirs and successors, will, give and grant unto the trustees of Queens College, in New Jersey, and their successors forever, that the said trustees from time to time, and forever hereafter, do elect, nominate, and appoint such a qualified person, being a member of the Dutch Reformed Church aforesaid, as they or the major part of any twelve of them, convened for that purpose, as above directed, shall think fit, to be the president of the said college." (*Charter of Queens College in New Jersey*, with Appendix, printed for the Trustees at New Brunswick.)[1]

New York: The original charter granted by George II to the trustees of the College of the Province of New York in 1754 states that in consideration of a gift of land from the " rector and inhabitants of the city of New York in communion of the Church of England, as by law established," etc., for the benefit of the college, " the president of the said college, for the time being shall forever hereafter be a member of and in communion with the Church of England," etc. (*Charters, Acts and Official Documents Relating to Columbia University*, compiled by John B. Pine, New York, 1895, p. 10-24.)

North Carolina: By an act of the legislature of North Carolina in 1766 incorporating a society for promoting and establishing a public school in Newbern it was provided that "no person shall be admitted to be master of the said school, but who is of the Established Church of England." (*Revisal of the Laws of North Carolina* 1773, p. 359-361.) In 1771 the legislature passed an act incorporating Queens College, in the town of Charlotte, Mecklinberg County, in which the following proviso with regard to the president appears: " And provided further that no person shall be admitted to be president of the said college but who is of the Established Church and who upon being nom-

[1] Quoted by Clews, p. 336.

inated and appointed by the fellows and trustees as aforesaid or the majority of them shall be duly licensed by the governor or commander-in-chief for the time being." (*Colonial Records* VIII, p. 486-490.)

The charter granted in 1708 to a public school in Philadelphia by William Penn, he being the proprietary governor of the colony, provided " that there should be forever thereafter fifteen discrete and religious persons of the people called Quakers, overseers of the same public school, to be incorporated and made one body politic and corporate — to have perpetual succession forever."[1] By the charter of 1711 the religious provision was broadened to the following: " Fifteen discreet and religious persons shall be overseers of the said school, who, with their successors, shall forever hereafter be one body politic and corporate in deed, name and law," etc.[2]

Rhode Island: In 1764 the legislature of Rhode Island passed an act incorporating the " Trustees and Fellows of the College or University of Rhode Island." The act specifically states this to be intended for a " liberal and catholic institution " and that no religious tests were ever to be admitted thereto. It is very evident, however, that this legislature's idea of what constituted liberality and catholicity and freedom from religious test as applied to a university was not the same as we of today, in our laws at least, conceive it to be. It provides that the members of all denominations of Protestants shall be eligible to any office in the university, except the presidency, which must always be filled by a Baptist, and in case he shall change his religious views after his election, the corporation is empowered to declare his place vacant. Thirty-three trustees were provided for, twenty-two of whom were to be Baptists, five Friends, five Episcopalians, and four Congregationalists, to hold office for life, and in case any one of them should see fit to change his religious views the corporation was empowered to remove him and substitute another in his place, taking care always to maintain the same proportion of membership in the various denominations named. The fellows were to be twelve in number of whom eight were to be Baptists and the rest indifferently of any or all denominations.

[1] Quoted by Wickersham, pp. 44-48.
[2] *Ibid.*

(*Records of the Colony of Rhode Island and 'Provincial Plantations in New England* VI, p. 385-391.)

South Carolina: In 1710 an act of the legislature of South Carolina for the founding and erecting of a free school provided: "And be it further enacted by the authority aforesaid, that the person to be master of the said school, shall be of the religion of the Church of England, and conform to the same, and shall be capable to teach the learned languages, that is to say, the Latin and Greek tongues, and also the useful parts of the mathematics." (*Statutes at Large of South Carolina* II, p. 342-346.) An act of 1712 providing for a free school in Charleston directed that the schoolmaster should always conform to the Church of England. (*Statutes at Large of South Carolina* II, p. 389-396.)

3. THE DELEGATION OF SUPERVISORY, ADMINISTRATIVE, OR TEACHING POWERS TO CHURCH AUTHORITIES

Occasionally a certain amount of control over education coupled with certain duties and authority in regard to enforcing school attendance, or in regard to the supervision of schools and education, is vested by law in the minister or some other church officer.

Connecticut: In a law enacted in Connecticut in 1659,[1] we find the school books subject to the approval of the ministers. In the law of 1676 it is the ministers who are recommended by the general court to look into the state of education in families, (*Connecticut Colonial Records* 1665-1676, p. 281) and in a law of 1680 it is the ministers who are urged to catechise the young people on the Sabbath days. (*Connecticut Colonial Records* 1678-1689, p. 65.)

Maryland: In the "Petitionary Act for Free Schools," enacted by the Maryland legislature in 1696, it was provided that the most reverend father in God, Thomas, by Divine Providence, Lord Archbishop of Canterbury, Primate and Metropolitan of all England, should be chancellor of the said schools. (*Bacon's Laws* 1686, Ch. XVII.)

Massachusetts: In 1641 the general court of Massachusetts

---

[1] Quoted in part on p. 8.

recommended that the elders should make out a catechism for the instruction of youth in the grounds of religion. (*Massachusetts Colonial Records* I, p. 328.)

New Netherlands: The ordinance of the Director-General and Council of New Netherlands for the better and more careful instruction of youth in the principles of the Christian religion, enacted in 1664,[1] provides for the examination of the children, by the teacher, in the presence of the ministers and elders.

Virginia: By an act of the legislature of Virginia passed in 1756, "the ministers, church wardens and vestrymen" of the parishes of Ware and Abingdon were constituted a body corporate by the name of the "Trustees and Governors of Peasley's Free School," whose duty it was and who had power to take over and manage certain property devised for the benefit of a free school, and to establish a free school in some convenient part of each of the parishes of Ware and Abingdon. (*Hening* VII, p. 41-43.) An act of 1759 constituted the ministers and church wardens of the parish of Elizabeth City together with the justices of the peace of the County of Elizabeth City, trustees and governors of Eaton's Charity School. (*Hening* VII, p. 317-320.)

The following instances of legislation in which some form of ecclesiastical control of education is provided for bear dates subsequent to 1776.

Georgia: The legislature of Georgia in 1785 enacted the following: "All officers appointed to the institution and government of the university shall be of the Christian religion; and within three months after they enter upon the execution of their trust shall publicly take the oath of allegiance and fidelity and the oaths of office prescribed in the statutes of the university; the president, before the governor or president of the council and all other officers before the president of the university." (*Act* Jan. 27, 1785, Sec. 9.) The Code of 1861, while still requiring all officers of the university to be of the Christian religion, omitted the provision regarding the taking of the oath, and provided against the exclusion of any one from the advantages of the institution on religious grounds. "All officers elected or

[1] Quoted in part on p. 19.

appointed for the university shall be of the Christian religion, but no person of any religious denomination shall be excluded from equal advantages of education and the immunities of the university on account of their speculative sentiments in religion or being of a different religious profession from the trustees or faculty." (*Code* 1861, Sec. 1127.)

Massachusetts: In Massachusetts a law of 1835 made it the duty of the ministers to enforce the school attendance: " It shall be the duty of the resident ministers of the gospel, the selectmen, and the school committees in the several towns, to exert their influence and use their best endeavors, that the youth of their towns shall regularly attend the schools established for their instruction." (*Revised Statutes* 1835, Pt. I, Title 10, Ch. 23, Sec. 8, Act of 1827, Ch. 143, Sec. 3.) The same provision is found in the General Statutes of 1859 (Ch. 38, Sec. II), and in the Public Statutes of 1882 (Ch. 44, Sec. 16.)

Minnesota: An act of the Minnesota legislature in 1867 amendatory to the act incorporating the Minnesota Central University, provides: " No religious tenet shall be required of any person to entitle him or her to all the privileges of the institution, but two-thirds of the board of trustees shall be connected with churches of the Baptist denomination." (*Act* March 9, 1867, IX, Sec. 4.)

New Mexico: In New Mexico the faculty of St. Michael's College in Santa Fe was authorized by the legislature to issue teachers' diplomas to all graduates of the college who might apply for the same. " Such diplomas shall be and the same are hereby considered as first class teachers' certificates in any and all counties of New Mexico to the same extent as diplomas or teachers' certificates issued by faculties of the territorial university," etc. (*Compiled Statutes* 1897, Par. 1625.) In the same volume we find the provision that the governor of the territory of New Mexico, his Grace the most reverend Archbishop of Santa Fe, and others shall be constituted a board of supervisors for the Orphans Home and Industrial School of the Territory of New Mexico, and it is made their duty to visit said institution from time to time and faithfully look after the moral and intellectual progress of the inmates. (*Compiled Statutes* 1897, Par.

1618.) There is also a provision that the Governor, the Superintendent of Public Instruction, the President of St. Michael's College of Santa Fe, etc., shall constitute a territorial board of education and exercise the powers and duties usually exercised by such boards. (*Compiled Statutes* 1897, Par. 1514.)

New York: The act of the New York legislature in 1784, establishing the University of New York after naming certain regents for the control of the university, proceeds: " and it shall and may be lawful to and for the clergy of the respective religious denominations in this state to meet at such time and place as they shall deem proper after the passing of this act, and being so met shall by a majority chuse and appoint one of their body to be a regent in the said university, and in case of death or resignation to chuse and appoint another in the same manner, and the regent so chosen and appointed shall have the like powers as any other regent appointed or to be appointed by virtue of this act." (*Session Laws* 1784, Ch. 51, Act May 1, 1784.) By an act of 1875 the sisterhood of Grey Nuns, an incorporation in the state of New York, was authorized, " to grant diplomas and honorary testimonials in such form and under such regulations as its board of trustees may determine, to any person who shall have or may hereafter be graduated from any seminary of learning of said corporation located within this state; and any such graduate to whom a diploma may be awarded may file such diploma or a duplicate thereof in the Department of Public Instruction, and the Superintendent of Public Instruction may thereupon in his discretion, issue a certificate to the effect that such a graduate is a qualified teacher of the common schools of this state." (*98th Session,* Ch. 353, Act May 15, 1875.)

South Carolina: In the Revised Statutes of South Carolina of 1873 appears the following with regard to the University of South Carolina: " The board of trustees shall take care that one of the professors provided for shall be a minister of the gospel, who shall also be charged with the duties of chaplain to said university, under such regulations and with such additional salary as may be fixed by said board." (*Revised Statutes* 1873, Ch. XLII, Sec. 14.) This wording is repeated in an act of the session of 1877-1878. (*Session Laws* 1877-1878, No. 492.)

CHAPTER IV

STATE SUPPORT OF SCHOOLS OWNED OR CONTROLLED BY THE CHURCH OR EXISTING FOR RELIGIOUS PURPOSES

In a number of the states the state legislatures have from time to time aided in the support of educational institutions more or less under the control of the church or existing for distinct religious purposes. This practice, begun by some of the Colonies, continued to be a fairly common feature of state legislation down to about the middle of the nineteenth century, straggling instances of the same occurring even later.

Sometimes this legislation takes the form of a direct grant of state money; again the income from some designated source will be set aside; still again it will be some item of equipment that the state will furnish to such institutions. Occasionally we find funds loaned by the state to religious bodies for the support of education. Very frequently when such grants are made, the state exacts in return that a certain number of students shall be educated free of all tuition charges in the schools so aided. Institutions controlled by ecclesiastical authority, and existing especially for charitable purposes, — orphans' homes, industrial schools, and the like — have been frequent beneficiaries of this practice. Sometimes where state funds are forbidden to be appropriated to educational institutions not under the exclusive control of the state, specific exceptions are made in favor of institutions having such charitable or benevolent designs.

As the states began to accumulate school funds from the sales of public lands and to provide the same from public taxation, along with the possibility of universal public education thus presented was the tendency to dissipate these funds among a large number of ecclesiastical claimants. Some of the specific instances of such diversion of public money, property, or credit to church-controlled educational institutions, it is the purpose of this chapter to indicate.

California: An act of 1870 appropriated state money to various charitable institutions. Among other items was one of $1500 to the St. Joseph Schools of Sacramento. (*Session Laws* 1869-1870, Ch. DXX, Act April 1, 1870.)

Connecticut: By an act of the legislature in 1715 there was appropriated to the trustees of the Collegiate School, Yale, whose religious purpose has already been indicated (p. 10) 500 pounds derived from the sale of public lands, to be used for building purposes. (*Connecticut Colonial Records* 1706-1716, p. 528-529.) In 1742 a grant of twelve pounds was made for repairing the school established by the Society for the Propagation of the Gospel, at Mohegan. (*Conn. Col. Rec.* VIII, p. 509.) A grant of twenty-five pounds was made in 1755 to provide dinners for the Indians at the school at Mohegan conducted by the Society for the Propagation of the Gospel. (*Conn. Col. Rec.* X, p. 384.) A grant of £40 was made in 1760 to pay the salary of the teacher of the Mohegan School conducted by the Society for the Propagation of the Gospel. (*Conn. Col. Rec.* XI, p. 414.) In 1766 a further grant of £15 was made to the teacher of the same school. (*Conn. Col. Rec.* 1762-1767, p. 485-486.)

Indiana: An act of 1855, while not specifically mentioning any religiously controlled school, nevertheless has its provisions broad enough to allow religiously controlled schools to share in the distribution of the public school funds. It reads in part as follows: " It shall be lawful for any such city or town to recognize any school, seminary or other institution of learning, which has been or may be erected by private enterprise, as a part of their system, and to make such appropriation of funds to such schools, seminary, or institution of learning, and upon such terms and conditions as may be deemed proper." (*Session Laws* 1855, Ch. LXXXVII, Act Mar. 5, 1855.)

Maryland: An act of the legislature in 1723 appropriated certain moneys to the visitors of certain county schools established for the training of youth for the service of the church and state and in which the masters were to be of the Church of England if such could be secured. (*Bacon's Laws* 1723, Ch. XIX.) By resolution adopted in 1818 the commissioners of the school fund of Baltimore County were required to pay over the school fund received by them, in such proportion as they should see fit, and as would most effectually promote the education of poor children in the city of Baltimore to the following: Union Board of Delegates Male Sabbath School Society of Baltimore, Female Union Society for the Promotion of Sabbath Schools in the City of Baltimore, Orphaline Charity School and such other institutions of a similar character in Baltimore as were or should be formed. (*Session Laws* 1818, Res. No. 24.) These societies and institutions reveal by their names their religious nature. The Orphaline Charity School was a Roman Catholic institution which was incorporated under the laws of the state in 1819. (*Act* Jan. 27, 1819.)

An act of 1826 made it the duty of the levy court to pay the share of Frederick County's distributive portion of the school fund belonging to the town of Frederickstown, in equal portions, to the president and directors of the Frederick Free School and to the pastor of St. John's Church in Frederickstown for the use of the Frederick Benevolent Female School, taking such security for the faithful application of the same as they should deem necessary. (*Act* Feb. 15, 1826.) Again in 1828 we find the legislature enacting the following: " Rev. John McElroy shall annually report to the superintendent of free schools in the City of Frederick the number of white minors within the taxable limits of Frederick, gratuitously educated in St. John's benevolent school. It is made the duty of the superintendent to pay to him a portion of the money raised for the establishment of free schools in Frederick equal to the amount paid for the same number of charity pupils who may be educated at any other free school in Frederick. Provided that in estimating the amount to be paid St. John's benevolent school the superintendent shall include the sum now paid annually, for the benefit of said school out of the school fund for Frederick County." (*Act* Feb. 9, 1828, Sec. 11.) Again in 1833 a legislative resolution directs the treasurer to pay Rev. John McElroy, principal of St. John's literary institution, $400 annually for the assistance of the same. Coupled with this grant is a declaration on the part of the legislature, in which it is declared to be the policy of the state to patronize and encourage establishments distinguished for general benevolence and unquestioned public utility. (*Resolution* No. 1, Jan. 17,

1833.) By a resolution adopted by the legislature in 1834 the Orphan's Court of Charles County was authorized to pay annually to the trustees of St. Paul's Chapel Free School in Charles County, $200 out of the Charles County share of the school fund, provided at least twenty-five poor children were educated during the preceding year before each donation. (*Resolution* No. 27, March 1, 1834.) A loan made by the state to St. Peter's Free School, Baltimore, in 1811, has an interesting history as revealed in the legislation of succeeding years. A resolution passed in 1818 regarding the same reads: "The loan hitherto made by the state to the trustees of St. Peter's Free School, Baltimore, is hereby continued for three years from the time the same became due." (*Session Laws* 1818, Res. No. 26, Dec., 1818.) In 1822 it was enacted that the loan made St. Peter's School in Baltimore by the state should be continued for three years from the time the same should become due, provided the interest should be paid annually. (*Session Laws* 1822, Res. No. 54, Feb. 23, 1822.) The next year a resolution was adopted releasing the trustees of St. Peter's School from payment of the interest upon the loan heretofore made to them by this state. (*Session Laws* 1823, Res. No. 24, Feb. 20, 1823.) In 1836 came the culmination, when the trustees of St. Peter's Free School, Baltimore, were released, exonerated, and discharged from the debt due by them to the state for monies advanced to them by virtue of Resolution No. 55, November session of 1811. (*Session Laws* 1836, Res. No. 4, January 29, 1836.)

Massachusetts: In 1654 the general court "besides the profit of the ferry formerly granted to the college, which shall be continued," orders "that there shall be yearly levied, by addition to the county rate, one hundred pounds, to be paid by the treasurer of the county to the college treasurer, for the behoof and maintenance of the president and fellows, to be distributed between the president and fellows according to the determination of the overseers of the college, and this to continue during the pleasure of the country." The religious purpose and control of Harvard College has already been sufficiently emphasized. The law making this grant, however, specifically mentions the religious purpose of the institution. (*Mass. Colonial Records*, IV, Pt. I, p. 205.)

Mississippi: In 1878 the legislature enacted the following: " When suitable school buildings and a library of two hundred bound volumes of well selected miscellaneous literature are furnished without expense to the state; and where a faculty of one or more teachers of good moral and educational standing in the state shall have associated themselves as a faculty in such school, students attending such school from any county in the state shall be entitled to draw from the school fund of his or her county, the pro rata amounts to which such student would have been entitled had he attended a first class public school in his own county." (*Session Laws* 1878, Ch. XX, Act Mar. 5, 1878.) The foregoing, while not specifically mentioning religious control, has its provisions broad enough to admit religiously controlled schools to share in the public school funds, and was for this reason declared unconstitutional in Otken *vs.* Lamkin. (See p. 151.)

New Hampshire: An act of the state legislature in 1845 donated to the New Hampshire Conference Seminary at Northfield, one of Carrigan's maps of New Hampshire. (*Session Laws* 1845, Ch. 283, Act June 26, 1845.) A similar donation was made to the Gilmanton Theological Seminary at Gilmanton in the same year. (*Session Laws* 1845, Ch. 284, Act July 2, 1845.)

New Jersey: An act passed in 1846 provided that if the patrons or proprietors of any school already organized under the care of any religious society or denomination of Christians were unwilling to relinquish such school, every such school should be entitled to receive its just and ratable share of the money assigned to the township out of the income of the school fund, and such additional sum as might be raised by or appropriated by the township for schools. (*Act* April 17, 1846.)

New Mexico: In the territory of New Mexico we find the following law: " The asylum of the Sisters of Charity of Santa Fe shall be constituted an orphans home and industrial school for the care, support, and education of the orphan and indigent children of the territory of New Mexico and to be known and legally designated as the Orphans Home and Industrial School of the Territory of New Mexico.

" Said orphans home and industrial school shall be under the care, charge, control and custody of the Sisters of Charity of Santa Fe, subject to the general supervision and orders of the board of supervisors hereby created.

" Said sisters of charity under whose care, custody and control said orphan and indigent children of the territory are hereby placed, are to board, clothe and instruct said children in the common school branches and shall receive as compensation therefor the sum of ten dollars per month for each child so boarded, clothed, instructed, and cared for."

The expense of the above to be defrayed out of the territorial treasury. (*Compiled Statutes* 1897, Par. 1617-1618, 1619-1620-1621.)

New York: New York's school legislation is especially rich in instances of public money being granted for the support of schools under the control of religious authorities or in which religious instruction is provided for. An act of 1801 provided that the mayor, aldermen, and commonalty of the City of New York should pay to the vestry of the Episcopal Church, the vestry of Christ's Church, the trustees of the First Presbyterian Church, the minister, elder, and deacons of the Reformed Dutch Church, and trustees of the Methodist Episcopal Church, the Scotch Presbyterian Church, the African School, the United German Lutheran Church, the German Reformed Churches, the First Baptist Church, and the United Brethren or Moravian Church, each one-eleventh part of all money remaining in their hands from the Acts of 1795 and 1799. The income from the said apportionment to be used for the education of poor children. (*Act* April 8, 1801.) By the Act of 1813 the commissioners of the school funds were to distribute the income from the same, plus an equal amount to be raised by tax on the city, to the trustees of the Free School Society, the trustees or treasurer of the Orphan Asylum Society, the Society of the Economical School in the city of New York, the African Free School, " and of such incorporated religious societies, in said city, as now support or hereafter shall establish charity schools," the distribution to be on the basis of the number of children from four to fifteen years of age taught free therein during the preceding year.

(*Laws* 36th session, Ch. LII, Act Mar. 12, 1813.) By a law of 1820 the commissioners were required to pay a share of the fund to the Roman Catholic Benevolent Society. (*Act* Apr. 1, 1820.) By a law of 1851 it was made lawful for any academy or high school, erected for literary, scientific, charitable or religious purposes, which had erected a building for high school purposes of the value of $2000 and which had complied with all the conditions prescribed by the law authorizing the regents to incorporate academies, to enjoy all the rights and privileges conferred by law on the academies of the state. One of these privileges was to share in the distribution of the literary fund. (*Session Laws* 1851, Ch. 544, Act July 11, 1851.)

Another act of 1851 appropriated out of the literary funds $250 each to Oneida Conference Academy, the Genesee Wesleyan Seminary, two institutions whose religious control is evidenced by their names. (*Session Laws* 1851, Ch. 291, Act June 25, 1851.) These grants were made under an existing law which provided for an annual donation from the literary fund to such academies as should instruct twenty persons at least in the art of teaching for a term of four months. These grants were to be limited to $250 per county. (*Session Laws* 1849, Ch. 175, Act Mar. 30, 1849, Sec. 2.) In 1852 a grant of $225 was made under the same law to the Oneida Conference Seminary. (*Session Laws* 1852, Ch. 161, Act Apr. 7, 1852.) An act of 1871 appropriated altogether $150,000 to a long list of orphan asylums, homes for the friendless, and other charitable institutions of like character. To the parochial school attached to the Church of St. Peter and St. Paul, Brooklyn, $750; to the parochial school attached to St. Joseph's Church, Brooklyn, $5000; to St. Patrick's Parochial School, Brooklyn, $375; etc. (*Session Laws* 1871, Ch. 869, Act Apr. 28, 1871.)

Pennsylvania: In 1789 an act was passed granting to the corporation of the ministers, trustees, elders, and deacons of the German Reformed Congregation in the City of Philadelphia certain lands for endowing a free school for the use of the poor of said congregation. (*Act* Sept. 23, 1789.) The following was passed at the legislative session of 1837-38: " When a free school of the common school grade shall be hereafter maintained in any accepting school district under the care and direction of a religious society it shall be lawful for the school directors to cause to be paid for the support of such school any portion of the school money not exceeding the ratable share of the taxable inhabitants whose children or apprentices shall be taught in the school.   Provided they shall think it not injurious to the common school of the district." (*Session Laws* 1837-38, No. 57.)   A similar law of 1849 provided that where a free school of the common grade should be under the care and direction of any religious society it was lawful for the directors of the district to cause to be paid to the proper person or persons for the support of the same any portion of the school funds of said district which they might deem just and reasonable not exceeding the ratable share of the inhabitants whose children or apprentices should attend the same.   Provided it was not considered injurious to the common school of the district, and be open to the visits of the directors of the district, and conform to the common school system of the state.   (*Session Laws* 1849, No. 316.)

Texas: In Texas we find the following enacted in 1874: " Provided, that in any school district where the trustees of said district find it impracticable for want of suitable buildings, or impossibility of obtaining teachers competent to instruct for the minimum price required by law, such trustees may contract with any private or public school of requisite qualifications for the instruction of all children within the scholastic age for the pro rata portion of the school fund, allowing such private or public schools the privilege of collecting their tuition fees exclusive of such pro rata portion of the school fund, from the parents or guardians of such children willing and able to pay." (*Session Laws* 1874, Ch. CLVI, Act May 2, 1874, Sec. 8.)   This seems to open a way for church-controlled schools to share in the distribution of public funds.

CHAPTER V

THE CLOSE ASSOCIATION OF EDUCATION AND RELIGION, THE SCHOOL AND THE CHURCH IN THE PUBLIC MIND

The wording of our laws very frequently reveals a close association in the public mind of education and religion, of the school and the church. Sometimes this is shown in a purely incidental fashion by reference to the use of a single building for both church and school purposes; at other times, provision will be made for the joint control of a church and a school by one corporate body; more frequently still, laws have been passed authorizing public schoolhouses to be used by religious denominations as places of religious worship.

In so far as such laws show a failure to differentiate distinctly the educational from the religious function, in so far as they reveal a tendency to combine the two, they deserve a place in our consideration of the secularization of education, as showing a condition and a tendency which must be overcome before complete secularization can prevail. So long as schools and churches are provided for in one building, so long as the state recognizes societies which exist for joint religious and educational purposes, so long as public school property is commonly used by church societies for religious worship, just so long may we expect the state to divide with the church, to a certain extent, educational control and educational purpose.

A dozen or more states still authorize in their laws the use of public school buildings under certain conditions and restrictions for holding denominational religious services. In nearly all the states it is a common practice, there being little prohibitory legislation. Such use of public property is a last remnant of that close union of the school and the church, of education and religion, which formerly prevailed so widely, and which subjected education so thoroughly to the control of the church, before the state began to assert its claims thereto.

Alabama: An act of the legislature of Alabama in 1866 provided for the repeal of an act permitting the sale of liquors within three miles of Friendship Church and Academy.   (*Session Laws* 1865-1866, No. 363, Act Jan. 26, 1866.)

Connecticut: In Connecticut the law of 1805 provided that " every town within this state wherein there is but one ecclesiastical society and wherein there are seventy householders or families or upwards, and every ecclesiastical society constituted, or that shall be constituted by the general assembly of the state, wherein there are the number of seventy householders or upward shall be at least eleven months in each year provided with and shall keep and maintain one good and sufficient school for the teaching and instructing of youth and children to read and write." (*Laws* 1805, p. 371.   Printed by Hudson and Goodwin.)   Again in 1838 we find: "All inhabitants living within the limits of ecclesiastical societies incorporated by law, shall constitute school societies." Power is given these when assembled in legal meeting to levy taxes, build and repair school houses and support schools, and to make any lawful agreement for such purposes. (*Revised Statutes* 1838, Title LXXXVIII, Ch. I, Sec. 1.)   This law seems to have continued in force till July 1, 1856, when the new law made towns responsible for schools.   An act of 1872 provides that " any school district or town may by a vote of two-thirds of those present at any legal meeting allow its school house or houses, when not in use for school purposes, to be used for any other purpose." (*Session Laws* 1872, Ch. LXXVII, Sec. 78, Act July 25, 1872.)   The same wording is found in the Revised Statutes of 1902, Section 2211.

Illinois: The legislature of Illinois in 1872 enacted a law giving the directors of any school district power to grant the temporary use of school houses, when not occupied by schools, for religious meetings and Sunday schools, for evening schools and literary societies and for such other purposes as they should deem proper.   (*Act* July 1, 1872, Sec. 39.)

Indiana: The legislature of Indiana in 1859 passed the following: " If a majority of the legal voters of any school district desire the use of the school house of such district for other purposes than common schools when unoccupied for common school purposes the trustees shall upon such application authorize the directors of such school district to permit the people of such district to use the house for any such purpose, giving equal rights and privileges to all religious denominations and political parties, without any regard whatever to the numerical strength of any religious denomination or political party of such district." (*Act* Mar. 3, 1859.) This law is repeated in the Annotated Statutes, Revision of 1894, Sec. 5999.

Kansas: "The district board shall have the care and keeping of the school house and other property belonging to the district. They are hereby authorized to open the school house for the use of religious, political, literary, scientific, mechanical, or agricultural societies belonging to the district for the purpose of holding the public meetings of said societies." (*General Statutes* 1901, Sec. 6194.) This is repeated in the General Statutes of 1905, Section 6716.

Maryland: By an act of the Maryland legislature in 1817 certain parties were authorized to draw a lottery for the purpose of raising funds for building an academy or school house and free church (one house) in or near Taney Town, Frederick County. (*Act* Jan. 16, 1817.) A few days later certain parties were authorized to draw a lottery for the purpose of purchasing land and erecting thereon a building to be used as a school and meeting house near Coxe's town. (*Act* Jan. 28, 1817.) An act of 1834 relating to the election of a board of trustees for Linganore School House and house of public worship provided that said house should be open and free for all Christian denominations to worship in, provided no one denomination should occupy it oftener than once in every two Sabbaths, and provided no meeting for public worship should interfere with the school hours except by consent of the trustees. (*Act* Feb. 17, 1834.)

Minnesota: An act of the Minnesota legislature reads as follows: "The trustees of any common school district may when petitioned therefor by a majority of the legal voters of the district permit and authorize the school house in their district to be used for purposes of divine worship, Sabbath schools, and such other purposes as in their judgment will not interfere with the use of the school house for school purposes." (*General Statutes*

1878, Vol. 2, Ch. 36, Par. 23a. Also Act Feb. 17, 1881, and *General Statutes* 1894, Sec. 3682.)

Mississippi: An act of the Mississippi legislature in 1840 incorporating Almucha Academy and Free Church provides: "The trustees may procure such house or houses as they may deem necessary, which house may be used for a place for religious worship for all Christian denominations at such times and under such regulations as may be prescribed by the trustees." (*Session Laws* 1840, Ch. 75, Act Jan. 27, 1840.)

Missouri: "Nothing in this section shall be so construed as to prevent the use of any school house for religious, literary, or other public purposes, or for the meeting of any farmer or labor organization or society for educational purposes, whether the same be secret or otherwise, when such use shall be demanded by a majority of the voters of such district voting at any annual or special meeting where such question was submitted." (*Revised Statutes* 1899, Sec. 9763.)

New Hampshire: "A school district or the school board thereof may grant the use of any school house in the district for a writing or singing school and for religious and other meetings whenever such use will not conflict with any regular school exercise." (*Public Statutes* 1901, Ch. 91, Sec. 18.)

North Dakota: It (District School Board) may permit a school house when not occupied for school purposes, to be used under careful restrictions for any proper purpose, giving equal rights and privileges to all religious denominations. (*Political Code* 1899, Sec. 700.)

Ohio: "When in the judgment of any board of education it shall be for the advantage of the children residing in any school district to hold literary societies, school exhibitions, singing schools, religious exercises, select or normal schools, the board of education shall authorize the opening of such school houses for the purposes aforesaid." (*Bates Annotated Statutes* 1906, Title III, Ch. 8, Sec. 3987.)

Oregon: The board (district) may, when authorized by a majority of the legal voters present and voting at the annual meeting called for that purpose, permit a school house when not occupied for school purposes to be used under careful restrictions for any proper purpose, giving equal rights and privileges to all religious denominations, etc. (*School Laws* 1907, p. 62, Sec. 119.)

Pennsylvania: By an act of the legislature in 1842 there was incorporated the Union Church and School Society of New Holland. The state treasurer was authorized to pay to the trustees of the same out of money remaining in the school fund, $200.00 for repairs, etc., to the building of which they were the trustees, and for the improvement of the means of education therein, provided, that should the district of Manchester adopt the common school system, the directors should be entitled to use the Union Church and school building free of charge. (*Session Laws* 1842, No. 89.)

South Carolina: An act of the legislature in 1850 declared the "church and school" at the Nation Ford a body corporate. (*Session Laws* 1850, No. 4005, Act of Dec. 20, 1850.)

Utah: The school district board may permit a school house when not occupied for school purposes to be used for any purpose which will not interfere with the seating or other furniture or property. (*Act* Mar. 13, 1890, Sec. 45. Also *Revised Statutes* 1898, Sec. 1822.)

West Virginia: "Trustees of sub-districts shall not without the permission of the district board of education allow said school houses to be used for any other purpose whatever except for the purpose of holding religious or literary meetings and Sunday-schools equally by the various religious denominations that may apply for the same." (*Code* 1887, Ch. 45, Sec. 15. Also *Code* 1906, Sec. 1587.)

Wisconsin: A majority of the district board of any school district in this state shall have the right to permit the school house to be occupied by religious meetings, temperance meetings, and any other meetings which in the judgment of the majority of the board will aid in disseminating intelligence and good morals among the inhabitants of the district. (*Act* Mar. 4, 1875, Sec. 1.) They may grant the request of any responsible inhabitant of the district to occupy the school house for such public meetings as will, in the judgment of the board, aid in disseminating good morals. (*Statutes* 1898, Sec. 435.)

CHAPTER VI

LAWS PROHIBITING RELIGIOUS INSTRUCTION AND THE ESTABLISHMENT OF DEPARTMENTS OF THEOLOGY

The colonial period of American educational history we have already shown to have been largely dominated by the religious purpose and aim of education. The period immediately succeeding, ending approximately with the middle of the nineteenth century, was in many respects an intermediate, a transition period in educational affairs. It was in this period that the necessity of education as a preparation for citizenship began to be felt with greater intensity on account of the multitudes of European immigrants who swelled our citizenship lists; it was in this period that the states, especially the rapidly developing middle-western states, rich in public land, began to respond with great liberality to the demand for educational funds and equipment; it was in this period that the problems involved by school systems and educational institutions, partly civic and partly religious in their aims and control, began to press themselves upon the American consciousness. The legislation of this period as a rule, in so far as it attempted to deal with these problems, was of a purely local nature. There was comparatively little state legislation in which the subject of religious instruction was mentioned. We have already shown that so far as favoring the religious element in education was concerned the state legislation of this period was confined to some half-dozen states; so far as opposing this element was concerned the state legislation of this period is confined to about the same number of states.

The full tide of the secularization movement is seen in the legislation enacted from about 1850 on.

The solutions of a legislative nature evolved to meet these problems took on a variety of forms. One feature is characteristic of practically all of this legislation — its negative, prohibitive nature. If there were no other evidence to show that prior to its enactment sectarian religious teaching had been common in the public schools, the stringent prohibition of the same in practically all of the states within a decade or two after 1850 would alone raise a suspicion that such had been a common practice even though few direct legal sanctions for the same were enacted after the close of the colonial period. It was not so much actual state legislation that this new legislation enacted in the period beginning about 1850 was repealing, so much as current practice which it was seeking to rectify.

The aim of education as set forth in this later legislation was civic, industrial, professional, not religious or ecclesiastical. Morality, character, knowledge, skill were emphasized, but to prepare leaders for the church, to supply a ministry, or to propagate the principles of the Christian religion no longer are mentioned as aims. Law schools, medical schools, normal schools, agricultural schools, and mechanical schools are provided for but no favorable mention is made of schools or departments of theology.

This legislation dealt with the nature of the instruction offered in the public schools, the establishment of theological departments in institutions of higher learning, especially those enjoying the privileges of incorporation, the nature of the text-books used, the establishment of religious tests, and ecclesiastical control of schools supported in whole or in part by the state. In this chapter I shall consider only that legislation which forbade religious, or sectarian religious instruction in the public schools, and the establishment of departments of theology in higher educational institutions.

Alabama: The Alabama Code of 1852 contains the following with regard to sectarian instruction in the University of Alabama: " No sectarian tenets or principles must be taught or inculcated at the university, by any officer or instructor therein." (*Code* 1852, Title XI, Ch. II, Sec. 851.) In 1854 an act to establish and maintain a system of free, public schools in Alabama, makes it the duty of the state superintendent of education, " to carefully guard that no sectarian religious views shall be inculcated in such schools." (*Session Laws* 1853-1854, No. 6, Act Feb. 15, 1854, Art. 2, Sec. 3.) In 1856 this duty is transferred from the state superintendent to the various county superintendents, of each one of whom it is made the duty, "to carefully guard that no sectarian religious views be taught in any free public school under his charge." (*Session Laws* 1855-1856, Art. 2, Sec. 9, Par. 4, Act Feb. 14, 1856.) Twenty years later in the code of 1876 the same wording is retained. (*Code* 1876, Title XI, Sec. 899, Par. 4.)

Arizona: In Arizona the legislature forbade in 1879 the teaching of any "sectarian or denominational doctrines" in the public schools, and declared that any school violating this provision should not receive any of the public school funds. (*Session Laws* 1879, No. 61, Sec. 38.) The law of 1883 in a similar prohibition uses the expression "sectarian doctrine," and provides the same penalty. (*Session Laws* 1883, No. 33, Sec. 62.) The law of 1895 in addition to repeating these provisions of the law of 1883 makes it the duty of the county school superintendent upon satisfactory evidence of the violation of this law by any school to withhold all apportionments of school moneys from said school. (*Revision* 1895, Ch. X, Sec. 88.) The law of 1901 contains the following with regard to instruction in the territorial university: "No sectarian tenets, opinions, doctrines, or principles shall be taught in any of the departments of said university," etc. (*Revised Statutes* 1901, Par. 3638.) The law of 1905 contains a different penalty for sectarian teaching from that usually employed. It provides that any teacher who shall "teach any sectarian doctrine or conduct any religious exercises in his school, . . . shall be deemed guilty of unprofessional conduct and it shall be the duty of the proper authority to revoke his or her certificate or diploma." (*Revised Laws* 1905, Sec. 112.)

California: The legislature of California in 1855 in an "Act to Establish, Support and Regulate Common Schools," provided as follows: "nor shall sectarian or denominational doctrines be taught therein; nor shall any school whatever receive any of the public school funds, which has not been taught in accordance with the provisions of this act." (*Session Laws* 1855, Ch. CLXXXV, Sec. 33, Act May 3, 1855.) The same act provides, with regard to incorporated cities and towns: "The common council on petition of fifty heads of white families, citizens of the district, shall establish a school or schools in said district and shall award said school or schools a pro rata of the school fund, provided no sectarian doctrines are taught in said school or schools," etc. (*Session Laws* 1855, Ch. CLXXXV, Sec. 22, Act May 3, 1855.) The law of 1870 provides as follows: "neither shall any sectarian or denominational doctrine be taught therein; and any school district, town, or city, the officers of which shall knowingly allow any schools to be taught in violation of these provisions shall forfeit all right to any apportionment of state or county school money," etc. (*Session Laws* 1869-1870, Ch. DLVI, Sec. 58, Act Apr. 4, 1870.)

Dakota: The legislature of the Territory of Dakota in 1887 enacted, that in cities, towns and villages, no sectarian doctrine should be taught or inculcated in any of the public schools, and provided that "no sectarian doctrine shall be taught in any public school." (*Political Code* 1887, Sec. 1829 and Sec. 1706.)

Idaho: In Idaho the law of 1907 with regard to the state university reads: "But no instruction either sectarian in religion or partisan in politics shall ever be allowed in any department of the University." (*School Laws* 1907, p. 10, Sec. 934.) ". . . any and every political, sectarian, or denominational doctrine is hereby expressly forbidden to be taught therein" (public schools). (*School Laws* 1911, Art. XXI, Sec. 186.)

Illinois: An act of the Illinois legislature passed in 1836 incorporating the Franklin Institute has the following section: "Provided however that nothing herein contained shall authorize the establishment of a theological department in said institution." (*Act* Jan. 18, 1836, Sec. 14.) Likewise with the Franklin Manual Labor College it was provided: "Nothing herein contained shall authorize the establishment of a theological department in said college." (*Act* Jan. 18, 1836, Sec. 4.)

Indiana: The Indiana legislature in 1853 enacted the following with regard to its school for the education of the deaf and dumb: "No sectarian tenets of religion shall be taught in such institution to any pupil thereof." (*Annotated Statutes Revised* 1894, Sec. 3070, Act May 6, 1853.) With regard to the state university it was enacted at the same date: "No sectarian ten-

ets shall be inculcated by any professor at such university."
(*Annot. St. Rev.* 1894, Sec. 6072.) In 1865 it was enacted with
regard to the state normal school: "A high standard of Christian morality shall be observed in the management of the school,
and as far as practicable be inculcated in the minds of the pupils;
yet no religious sectarian tenets shall be taught." (*Annot. St.
Rev.* 1894, Sec. 6045.)

Kansas: The legislature of Kansas in 1876 enacted with
regard to cities of the first and second class that no sectarian or
religious doctrine should be taught or inculcated in any of the
public schools therein. (*General Statutes* 1905, Sec. 6816 and
6850, Act April 7, 1876.)

Kentucky: The legislature of Kentucky in 1893 enacted the
following with regard to the Colored Normal School: "No
religious tenets shall be taught in said normal school, but a high
standard of Christian morality shall be observed in its management, and so far as practicable, shall be inculcated in the minds
of the pupils." (*Statutes* 1903, Sec. 4532, Act May 22, 1893.)
With regard to the common schools an act of 1893 provides:
"nor shall any sectarian, infidel, or immoral doctrine be taught
therein." (*Statutes* 1903, Sec. 4368, Act July 6, 1893.)

Louisiana: The legislature of Louisiana in 1855 forbade
"any course of religious instruction (to) be taught or allowed
of a sectarian character and tendency" in the state university.
(*Revised Statutes* 1870, Sec. 1358, Acts 1855, No. 320, Sec. 8.)

Maine: The Revised Statutes of Maine for 1903 contain the
following in regard to state normal schools: "Such schools
while teaching the fundamental truths of Christianity, and the
great principles of morality, recognized by law, shall be free
from all denominational teachings," etc. (*Revised Statutes*
1903, Ch. 15, Sec. 109, Par. IV.)

Michigan: The Compiled Laws of Michigan for 1897 contain
the following: "No school district shall apply any of the money
received by it from the primary school interest fund or from
any and all other sources for the support of any school of a sectarian character, whether the same be under the control of any
religious society or made sectarian by the school district board."
(*Compiled Laws* 1897, Par. 4676.)

Minnesota: The School Laws of Minnesota for 1907 forbid the teaching of "anything sectarian" in the state university. (*School Laws* 1907, p. 130, Sec. 322.)

Missouri: An act of the Missouri legislature in 1835 reads in part as follows: "In all schools established according to the provisions of this act there shall be taught reading, writing, arithmetic, geography, English grammar, and such other branches of education, (theology excepted) as the funds may justify." (*Act* Mar. 19, 1835, Sec. 35.)

Montana: The legislature of Montana in 1872 enacted as follows: "neither shall any political, sectarian, or denominational doctrine be taught therein; and any school district the officers of which shall knowingly allow any school to be taught in violation of these provisions shall forfeit all right to any county apportionment of school moneys, and upon satisfactory evidence of such violation the county superintendent shall withhold its county apportionment. (*Session Laws* 1872, Ch. LXXXVIII, Sec. 35, Act Jan. 12, 1872.) The above provision is repeated in the Compiled Statutes of 1887, Sec. 1893. An act of 1893 regarding the state university provides: "No instruction, either sectarian in religion or partisan in politics shall ever be allowed in any department of the university." (*Pol. Code* 1895, Sec. 1545, Act Feb. 17, 1893.) The law of 1895 increases the penalty for violation of the anti-sectarian law. "Nor must any sectarian or denominational doctrine be taught therein. Any school district the officers of which knowingly allow any school to be taught in violation of these provisions forfeits all rights to any state or county apportionment of school moneys; and upon satisfactory evidence of such violation, the superintendent of public instruction and the county superintendent must withhold both state and county apportionments." (*Pol. Code* 1895, Sec. 1863, Act Mar. 11, 1895.)

Nebraska: In an act relative to schools in the city of Omaha the legislature of Nebraska provided as follows: "No sectarian or religious doctrines shall be taught or inculcated in any of the public schools of said city." (*Session Laws* 1870-1871, p. 177, Act June 6, 1871.) The act of 1875 relating to public schools in cities of the second class provided: "No sectarian or religious doctrine shall be taught or inculcated in any of the public schools of any district contemplated in this act." (*Session Laws* 1875, p. 208, Act Feb. 25, 1875, Sec. 20.)

Nevada: In Nevada the General Statutes of 1885 contained the following: "nor shall sectarian or denominational doctrines be taught therein (public schools); nor shall any school whatever receive any of the public school funds which has not been taught in accordance with the provisions of this act." (*General Statutes* 1885, Sec. 1338.) The Compiled Laws of 1900, Sec. 1323, contain this same provision.

New Mexico: In New Mexico the Compiled Laws of 1897 contain a provision that no sectarian doctrine shall be taught or inculcated in any of the public schools of any city or town of the territory. (*Compiled Laws* 1897, Par. 1582.)

New York: An act of the New York State legislature relative to schools in New York City, passed in 1842, reads as follows: " No school above mentioned, or which shall be organized under this act, in which any religious, sectarian doctrine shall be taught, inculcated or practiced, shall receive any portion of the school moneys to be distributed as hereinafter provided; and it shall be the duty of the trustees, inspectors, and commissioners of schools in each ward, and of the deputy superintendent of schools, from time to time and as frequently as need be, to examine and ascertain, and report to the said board of education whether any religious sectarian doctrine or tenet shall have been taught, inculcated or practiced in any of the schools in their respective wards." (*65th Session,* Ch. 150, Sec. 14, Act April 11, 1842.) The act of 1844 makes a slight change in the wording of this prohibition: " But no school shall be entitled to a portion of the school moneys in which the religious sectarian doctrine or tenet of any particular Christian, or other religious sect shall be taught, inculcated or practiced," etc. (*67th Session,* Ch. 320, Sec. 12, Act May 7, 1844.) This was repeated in 1846 (*Revised Statutes* 1846, Pt. 1, Ch. XV, Sec. 208), in 1851 (*74th Session,* Ch. 386, Sec. 18, Act July 3, 1851), and in 1882 (*105th Session,* Ch. 410, Sec. 1062, Act July 1, 1882.) By the act of 1844 it is made the duty of the county superintendent in the City of New York; " To examine and ascertain and report to the board of education whether any of the provisions of the act in relation to religious sectarian teaching . . . have been violated in any of the schools in the different wards of the city." (*67th Session,* Ch. 320, Sec. 44, Act May 7, 1844.)

This provision was repeated in the act of 1851 (*74th Session,* Ch. 386, Sec. 11, Act July 3, 1851.) An act of 1850 relative to the schools of Brooklyn reads: " No school in said city shall be entitled to any portion of the school moneys in which the religious sectarian doctrine or tenets of any particular Christian or other religious sect shall be taught or inculcated," etc. (*73rd Session,* Ch. 143, Sec. 19, Act April 4, 1850.) An act applicable to the City of New York passed in 1851 and amended in 1853 and 1854 reads as follows: " No school shall be entitled to, or receive any portion of the school monies, in which the religious doctrines or tenets of any particular Christian or other religious sect shall be taught, inculcated, or practiced," etc. (*Act* July 3, 1851, as amended June 4, 1853, Mar. 31, 1854, and April 15, 1854.) An act of 1854 made it the duty of the superintendent in New York City to examine, ascertain and report to the board of education whether the provisions of the act in relation to sectarian teaching, etc., have been violated in any of the schools of the city. (*77th Session,* Ch. 101, Sec. 11, Act Mar. 31, 1854.) An act of 1864 made it the duty of the inspectors of common schools to report any violation of the law in respect to teaching sectarian doctrines, etc. (*Act* April 25, 1864.)

North Dakota: The Political Code of North Dakota for 1899 contains the following with regard to the state university: " But no instruction either sectarian in religion or partisan in politics shall ever be allowed in any department of the university." (*Pol. Code* 1899, Sec. 881.)

Oklahoma: The territorial legislature of Oklahoma in 1890 enacted the following with regard to the university: " The board of regents shall determine the moral and educational qualifications of applicants for admission to the various courses of instruction, but no instruction either sectarian in religion or partisan in politics shall ever be allowed in any department of the university." (*Revised and Annotated Statutes* 1903, Ch. 77, Art. 17, Sec. 6384, Act Dec. 19, 1890.) In an act of 1895, entitled "An act to Create and Maintain Union or Graded School Districts," we find: " No sectarian doctrine shall be taught or inculcated in any of the public schools of the union district," etc. (*Rev. and Annot. St.* 1903, Ch. 77, Art. 8, Sec. 6247, Act Feb. 19, 1895.) In the School Laws of 1901-02 we find the following with regard to cities of the first class: " No sectarian doctrine shall be taught or inculcated in any of the public schools of the city," etc. (*School Laws* 1901-02, Art. IX, Sec. 20.) The same is repeated in the Revised and Annotated Statutes of 1903, Ch. 77, Art. 9, Sec. 6267. In the School Laws of 1901-02 we find: " No sectarian or religious doctrines shall be taught or inculcated in any of the public schools in this territory," etc. (*School Laws* 1901-02, Art. IV, Sec. 25.) The Revised and Annotated Statutes of 1903, Ch. 77, Art. 3, Sec. 6189, contain the same, as do also the School Laws of 1908 except that in the latter " territory " becomes " state."

South Carolina: The Session Laws of South Carolina for 1870-1871 contain an "Act to Establish and Maintain a System of Free Common Schools for the State of South Carolina," which makes it the duty of the state superintendent of schools to forbid sectarian or partisan instruction in the schools. (*Session Laws* 1870-1871, No. 346, Sec. 10.) This is repeated in the Revised Statutes of 1873, Ch. XXXV, Sec. 5, the Session Laws of 1877-1878, No. 516, Sec. 11, the Revised Statutes of 1894, Sec. 1034, and the Code of 1902, Sec. 1175. On page 25 we have already noted an act of 1865 with regard to the University of South Carolina providing for the establishment therein of a " school of mental and moral philosophy, sacred literature, and evidences of Christianity " as one of the departments. (*Session Laws* 1864-1865, p. 313, No. 4748.) At the session of 1877-1878 an act was passed which authorized and required the board of trustees of the University to organize each branch of the University by establishing such schools in each of them and prescribing such courses and mode of instruction therein as they may think fit, and by electing competent professors and tutors of the several schools, governing themselves in the number of schools and of the professors in each branch of said university by the requirements and necessities of each. (*Session Laws* 1877-1878, Act No. 492, Sec. 13.) No mention is here made of sacred literature and evidences of Christianity as in the earlier law. The only restriction as to the departments to be established, is one requiring the establishment of an agricultural department in said university. (*Ibid.* Sec. 25.)

South Dakota: The Political Code of South Dakota contains the following with regard to the state university : " No instruction either sectarian in religion or partisan in politics shall ever be allowed in any department of the University." (*Pol. Code* 1903, Sec. 578.) In the Code of 1903 under the title, " Cities, Towns, and Adjacent Territory, Organized as Independent Districts " is the following : " No sectarian doctrine may be taught or inculcated in any of the schools of the corporation," etc. (*Pol. Code* 1903, Sec. 2423.)

Texas: By an act of the Texas legislature passed in 1870, teachers conducting private schools might under certain conditions be contracted with, by boards of trustees, to instruct the children of the district, but subject to the following : " and provided further that no sectarian doctrine shall be taught in said private schools." (*12th Legislative Session,* Ch. LXVIII, Act Aug. 13, 1870.) The law of 1876 is a very strict one : " No school in which sectarian religion is taught shall be entitled to any portion of the available school fund, nor shall any form of religion be taught in any public free school in this state." (*Session Laws* 1876, Ch. 120, Sec. 16, Act Aug. 19, 1876.) The act of 1881 establishing the state university provided that no course of instruction of a sectarian character should be taught therein. (*Session Laws* 1881, Ch. 75, Act Mar. 30, 1881.) The Revised Statutes of 1895 contain the same provision. (*Revised Statutes* 1895, Art. 3853.)

Utah: The legislature of Utah in 1892 enacted the following : " No atheistic, infidel, sectarian, or denominational doctrine shall be taught in any of the district schools of the state. Moral instruction, tending to impress upon the minds of pupils the importance of good manners, truthfulness, temperance, purity, patriotism and industry shall be given in every district school." (*Act* Mar. 10, 1892, Sec. 65.) The Revised Statutes of 1898 modify this slightly : " No atheistic, infidel, sectarian, religious, or denominational doctrine shall be taught in any of the district schools of this state. Moral instruction tending to impress upon the minds of the pupils the importance of good manners, truthfulness, temperance, purity, patriotism, and industry shall be given in every district school," etc. (*Revised Statutes* 1898, Sec. 1848.)

Virginia: An act of the legislature of Virginia passed in 1839, " Concerning Devises made to Schools, Academies and Colleges," provided " that nothing in this act contained shall be so construed as to give validity to any devise or bequest to any theological seminary." (*Session Laws* 1839, Ch. 12, Sec. 7, Act Apr. 2, 1839.) The purpose of such a law as this was no doubt to prevent undue influence being brought to bear by representatives of the church upon those about to make their wills. A series of acts by the legislature of this state incorporating Richmond College (*Session Laws* 1840, Ch. 115, Sec. 8, Act Mar. 4, 1840) ; Bethany College (*Session Laws* 1840, Ch. 116, Sec. 14, Act Mar. 2, 1840) ; Northwestern Academy (*Session Laws* 1841-2, Ch. 147, Sec. 9, Act Mar. 26, 1842) ; Marshall Academy (*Session Laws* 1844-1845, Ch. 119, Sec. 12, Act Feb. 21, 1845) ; Virginia Collegiate Institute (*Session Laws* 1844-45, Ch. 120, Sec. 4, Act Jan. 20, 1845) ; Shenandoah College (*Session Laws* 1848-9, Ch. 237, Sec. 14, Act Feb. 21, 1849) ; and Roanoke College (*Session Laws* 1852-3, Ch. 344, Sec. 9, Act Mar. 14, 1853), forbade the establishment of any theological professorship or theological school in said institutions. An act of 1847 amending the Act of Feb. 25, 1846, for the counties of Londonn, Fairfax, and Kanawha, provides that no instruction shall be given in the public schools calculated to favor the doctrinal tenets of any religious sect or denomination. (*Session Laws* 1846-7, Ch. 33, Sec. 5, Act Mar. 10, 1847.) Another law of this state passed in 1850 incorporating the Academy of Visitation provided that : " Nothing herein contained shall be construed or taken as at any time to authorize the establishment of a nunnery or a theological professorship in or connected with said academy." (*Session Laws* 1849-50, Ch. 192, Sec. 9, Act Mar. 14, 1850.)

Washington: The legislature of Washington enacted the following in 1883 with regard to its common schools : " Neither shall any political, sectarian, denominational, or infidel doctrine be taught therein; and any teacher who shall violate these provisions shall forfeit his permit or certificate for the period of one year." (*Act* No. 28, 1883, Title IX, Sec. 53.)

Wisconsin: The legislature of Wisconsin in 1880 passed a law amending the act of 1854 by which the German and English Academy in Milwaukee was incorporated. This provides that no sectarian instruction whatever shall be given in said school. (*Session Laws* 1880, Ch. 61, Sec. 1, Act Feb. 28, 1880.) With regard to the state university of Wisconsin we find the following in the statutes for 1898: " But no instruction either sectarian in religion or partisan in politics shall ever be allowed in any department of the university." (*Wisconsin Statutes* 1898, Sec. 381.)

Wyoming: The legislature of Wyoming enacted in 1886 the following with regard to the state university: " No sectarian tenets or principles shall be taught, instructed, or inculcated at said university by any president, professor or tutor therein." (*Session Laws* 1886, Ch. 37, Sec. 45.) In 1899 the Revised Statutes read: " But no instruction either sectarian in religion or partisan in politics shall ever be allowed in any department of the university," etc. (*Revised Statutes* 1899, Sec. 491, *Session Laws* 1890-91, Ch. 75, Sec. 6, Act Jan. 10, 1891.) With regard to its agricultural college the following was enacted in 1891: " No sectarian tenets or principles shall be taught, instructed or inculcated at said institution, by any president, professor or tutor therein." (*Session Laws* 1890-91, Ch. 92, Sec. 11, Act Jan. 10, 1891.) The same is repeated in the Revised Statutes of 1899, Sec. 513.

CHAPTER VII

LAWS FORBIDDING THE USE OF SECTARIAN TEXT-BOOKS

Closely related to legislation forbidding the teaching of sectarian or denominational religious tenets, is legislation forbidding the use of text-books in which such tenets are either favored or opposed. With the adoption of uniform series of text-books, often for a whole state, embracing sections of widely divergent religious opinion, such laws became essential to the welfare of the public schools.

So long as each individual community could determine for itself what books should be used in its school, a certain amount of adaptation to individual community desires in religious matters was possible. The religion of the majority, at least, in each community, if there was a decisive majority, could be favored. But centralization and the accompanying requirements of uniformity, with which American school legislation abounds, made this no longer possible. In most of the states, text-books for state-wide or county-wide use are today adopted by state or county authorities. With the provision for such centralized authority, has come about legislation forbidding the use of books in which any particular religious tenets are either favored or opposed.

One Book very commonly used in the schools of practically all the states has been the Holy Bible. Frequently books containing extracts therefrom have been used for reading purposes. A common practice has been for the teacher to read a portion therefrom as a part of the opening exercises each day of school. Sometimes responsive readings therefrom by teacher and pupils have been employed. Very often objection has been raised by those of different religious views from those dominant in particular communities, against having their children forced to read or listen to the reading of the particular version of the Bible employed in the schools where they attended, or of any version whatever, or of books containing extracts therefrom. The contest over the use of this book has been one of the most widespread, longest continued, and most bitter in which our people have engaged.

Two general lines of policy can be detected in state legislation dealing therewith; one forbidding the use of any sectarian books, leaving it to the courts to determine in any particular case whether or not a book is sectarian; the other, either forbidding sectarian books or not, but in either case providing that the Bible shall not be so considered nor excluded. Sometimes under this second policy the law has left the reading of the Bible to the option of the individual community, or to the teacher of the school. No law has ever been passed by any state legislature specifically forbidding the use of the Bible in the schools. Sometimes it is provided that the Bible shall be read by the teacher for a certain number of minutes daily, without written note or oral comment thereon. Again we find a proviso that children whose parents object to their being present while the Bible is being read shall be excused from attendance on the reading thereof. The common method of securing compliance with these laws is, as with those forbidding sectarian instruction, to threaten to withhold the state school funds.

To the first policy named, by far the most general, that forbidding the use of any sectarian books, leaving it to the courts to determine in any particular case whether or not a book is sectarian, belong the following laws:

Alabama: An act of the legislature of Alabama passed in 1903 to create a text-book commission and to procure a uniform series of text-books, provided that none of said books should contain anything of a partisan or sectarian character. (*General Public School Laws* 1908, Sec. 1811, Act Mar. 4, 1903.)

Arizona: "No books, tracts or papers of a sectarian or denominational character shall be used or introduced in any school established under the provisions of this act, . . . nor shall any school whatever receive any of the public school funds which has not been taught in accordance with the provisions of this act." (*Session Laws* 1879, No. 61, Sec. 38.) "It shall be the duty of the Board of Trustees to exclude from schools and school libraries all books, publications or papers of a sectarian, partisan or immoral character." (*Session Laws* 1883, No. 33, Sec. 10.) The law of 1883 contained the same provisions as that of 1879 above quoted. (*Session Laws* 1883, No. 33, Sec. 62.) In the revision of 1895 the wording of the penalty attached is slightly changed. " No books, tracts or papers of a sectarian character shall be used or introduced into any school established under the provisions of this title . . . nor shall any school whatever . . . which has not been taught in accordance with the provisions of this title, receive any of the public school funds, and upon satisfactory evidence of such violation the county superintendent must withhold all apportionment of school moneys from said school." (*Revision* 1895, Ch. X, Sec. 88.) "Any teacher who shall use any sectarian or denominational books . . . in his school . . . shall be deemed guilty of unprofessional conduct and it shall be the duty of the proper authority to revoke his or her certificate or diploma." (*Revised Laws* 1905, Sec. 112.) " It shall be the duty of the board of trustees to exclude from schools and school libraries all books, publications or papers of a sectarian, partisan, or denominational character." (*School Laws* 1908, Ch. VI, Sec. 50, Par. 13.)

Arkansas: " No teacher employed in any of the common schools shall permit sectarian books to be used as a reading or text-book in the school under his care." (*Digest* 1874, Sec. 5453, Act April 29, 1873, Sec. 52.) This law is repeated in the Digest of 1884, Sec. 6244.

California: "An act to Establish, Support and Regulate Common Schools: No books, tracts or papers of a sectarian or denominational character shall be used or introduced in any school established under the provisions of this act: — nor shall any school whatever receive any of the public school funds, which has not been taught in accordance with the principles of this act." (*Session Laws* 1855, Ch. CLXXXV, Sec. 33, Act May 3, 1855.) " Trustees may receive donations of books, maps or charts from any person; provided, no books of a sectarian character shall be placed in the library, and that any such books found therein shall be removed by order of the county superintendent." (*Session Laws* 1869-70, Ch. DLVI, Sec. 73, Act April 4, 1870.)

The same law makes it the duty of the state board of education to prepare a list of books suitable for school libraries, in which no work of a sectarian character shall be included, etc. (*Session Laws* 1869-70, Ch. DLVI, Sec. 71, Act April 4, 1870.) The same law specifies among the powers and duties of boards of trustees and boards of education, to exclude from schools and school libraries all books, tracts, papers, or catechisms of a sectarian character. (*Session Laws* 1869-70, Ch. DLVI, Sec. 11, Act April 4, 1870.) " No books, tracts, papers, catechisms or other publications of a sectarian or denominational character shall be used or distributed in any school or shall be made a part of any school library . . .; and any school district, town, or city, the officers of which shall knowingly allow any schools to be taught in violation of these provisions shall forfeit all right to any apportionment of state or county school money," etc. (*Session Laws* 1869-70, Ch. DLVI, Sec. 58, Act April 4, 1870.)

Colorado: Among the powers of school directors enumerated in the General Statutes of 1883 are : " To exclude from schools and school libraries all books, tracts, papers or catechisms of a sectarian character." (*General Statutes* 1883, Ch. XCVII.)

Idaho: It is made the duty of trustees in Independent school districts, " To exclude from the schools and school libraries of said districts, all books, tracts, papers and catechisms of a sectarian nature." (*School Laws* 1907, p. 82, par. 10.) " No books, papers, tracts or documents of a political, sectarian or denominational character shall be used or introduced in any school established under the provisions of this Chapter . . . nor shall any teacher or any district receive any of the public school moneys in which the schools have not been taught in accordance with the provisions of this Chapter." (*School Laws* 1911, Art. XXI, Sec. 186.)

Indiana: In an act passed in 1889 providing for the selection of a series of text-books by the state board of education we find : " Provided, that none of said text books shall contain anything of a partisan or sectarian character." (*Annotated Statutes Revision* 1894, Sec. 5853. Acts 1889, Ch. L, Sec. 1, p. 74.)

Kansas: " Provided, that no text-books shall be adopted that contain anything of a partisan or sectarian character." (*General Statutes* 1905, Sec. 7908, Act March 19, 1897, Ch. 179, Sec. 4.)

Kentucky: "No books or other publications of a sectarian, infidel, or immoral character shall be used or distributed in any common school," etc. (*Statutes* 1903, Ch. 113, Sec. 4368, Act July 6, 1893.) With regard to the County Board of Examiners the law specifies: "The said board shall not adopt any text-books of an immoral, sectional or sectarian character for use in the common schools." (*Statutes* 1903, Ch. 113, Sec. 4423.) With regard to district libraries we find: "But no books of a sectarian, infidel, or immoral character shall be placed in the library; and any such books found therein shall be removed by order of the trustees or the county superintendent." (*Statutes* 1903, Sec. 4521.) "No teacher employed in any of the common schools shall permit sectarian books to be used as a reading or text-book in the school under his care." (*Statutes* 1904, Sec. 7654.)

Maryland: "School books shall contain nothing of a sectarian or partisan character." (*Session Laws* 1872, Ch. X, Sec. 1, Act April 1, 1872.)

Massachusetts: "The school committee shall never direct to be purchased or used, in any of the town schools, any school books which are calculated to favor the tenets of any particular sect of Christians." (*Session Laws* 1827, Ch. 143, Sec. 7, Act March 10, 1827.) The same is found in the Revised Statutes for 1835, Pt. I., Tit. 10, Ch. 23, Sec. 23.

Mississippi: In the Code of 1892 there is enumerated among the duties of trustees of separate school districts: "To exclude from schools and school libraries all books, publications, or papers of a sectarian, partisan, denominational or immoral character." (*Annotated Code* 1892, Sec. 4006.) "Provided that none of said text-books so selected or adopted shall contain anything of a partisan or sectarian character." (*School Laws* 1906, p. 4, Sec. 4595.)

Montana: "No books, tracts, papers, catechisms or other publications of a partisan, sectarian or denominational character, shall be used or distributed in any school; and any school district, the officers of which shall knowingly allow any school to be taught in violation of these provisions shall forfeit all right to any county apportionment of school moneys, and upon satisfactory evidence of such violation the county superintendent shall withhold its county apportionment." (*Session Laws* 1872, Ch. LXXXVIII, Sec. 35, Act Jan. 12, 1872.) The above is repeated in the Compiled Statutes of 1887, Sec. 1893. Section 27 of the same law reads as follows: "Every board of trustees unless otherwise especially provided, shall have power and it shall be their duty: To exclude from schools and school libraries all books, tracts, papers or catechisms of a sectarian or political character." (*Session Laws* 1872, Ch. LXXXVIII, Sec. 27, Act Jan. 12, 1872.) An act of 1895 reads as follows: "No publication of a sectarian, partisan, or denominational character must be used or distributed in any school or be made a part of any school library; . . . Any school district, the officers of which knowingly allow any school to be taught in violation of these provisions, forfeits all right to any state or county apportionment of school moneys; and upon satisfactory evidence of such violation, the superintendent of public instruction and the county superintendent must withhold both state and county apportionments." (*Political Code* 1895, Sec. 1863, Act March 11, 1895.)

Nevada: "No books, tracts or papers of a sectarian or denominational character shall be used or introduced in any school established under the provisions of this act; . . . nor shall any school whatever receive any of the public school funds which has not been taught in accordance with the provisions of this act." (*General Statutes* 1885, Sec. 1338.) This provision is repeated in the Compiled Laws of 1900, Sec. 1323.

New Hampshire: "No book shall be directed to be used as a school book which is calculated to favor any particular religious or political sect or tenet." (*Revised Statutes* 1842, Ch. 73, Sec. 12.) The Compiled Statutes of 1853, Ch. 77, Sec. 13, contains the same provision. In 1895 the following was adopted: "No book shall be introduced into the public schools calculated to favor any particular religious sect or political party." (*Session Laws* 1895, Ch. 50, Sec. 5.) This is repeated in the Public Statutes of 1901, Ch. 92, Sec. 9.

New York: The following provision applies to the schools of New York City only: " But no such school shall be entitled to a portion of such moneys . . . in which any book or books containing any sectarian composition shall be used in the course of instruction. . . ." (*Laws of 66th Session,* Ch. 216, Sec. 15, Act April 18, 1843.)

North Carolina: " The state board of education may recommend the course of study to be pursued, the text-books, and other means of instruction to be used in the public schools: Provided, that no sectarian or political text-books or influences shall be used in any public school." (*Revisal* 1873, Ch. 68, Sec. 59.) " The state board of education shall recommend a series of text-books to be used in the public schools for a term of three years and until otherwise ordered . . .; Provided further, no sectarian or political books shall be used in the public schools." (*Code* 1883, Vol. 2, Ch. 15, Sec. 2539. Act 1881, Ch. 200, Sec. 9.) " None of such text-books shall contain anything of a partisan or sectarian character, and all shall be written or printed in English." (*Revisal* 1905, Sec. 4060.)

North Dakota: An act of 1891 under the duties of district school boards provides as follows: " But it shall exclude therefrom (school library) all books unsuited to the cultivation of good character and good morals and manners, and no sectarian publication devoted to the discussion of sectarian differences and creeds shall be admitted to the library." (*Political Code* 1899, Sec. 694, Acts 1891, Ch. 56, Sec. 14.)

Oklahoma: In an act of 1908 providing for state uniformity of books, etc., we find the following: " Provided, that none of said text-books shall contain anything of a partisan or sectarian character." (*Laws* 1908, No. 331, Art. XXXII, Sec. 2.)

South Carolina: An act passed by the legislature of 1870-71 amending an act to " Establish and Maintain a System of Free Common Schools for the State of South Carolina," specifies as one of the duties of the state superintendent of schools: " He shall forbid the use of sectarian or partisan books and instruction in schools." (*Session Laws* 1870-71, No. 346, Sec. 10.) The above is repeated in Revised Statutes of 1873, Ch. XXXV,

Sec. 5; Session Laws of 1877-78, No. 516, Sec. 11; Revised Statutes of 1894, Sec. 1034; and Code of 1902, Sec. 1175.

Tennessee: In 1899 the following was enacted with regard to a uniform series of text-books: " Provided, that none of said text-books shall contain anything of a partisan or sectarian character." (*Session Laws* 1899, Ch. 205, Act April 13, 1899.)

Virginia: An act of 1847 to amend for the counties of Londonn, Fairfax, and Kanawha, the act of February 25, 1846, establishing Free Schools, provides: " No books shall be used nor instruction given in the public schools calculated to favor the doctrinal tenets of any religious sect or denomination." (*Session Laws* 1846-7, Ch. 33, Sec. 5, Act March 10, 1847.) An act of 1847 amending an act of. Feb. 25, 1846, establishing Free Schools in the counties of Frederick and Jefferson provides: " No books of an immoral or irreligious tendency, and none of a strictly sectarian character shall be used therein." (*Session Laws* 1846-7, Ch. 32, Sec. 9, Act March 20, 1847.) An act of 1849 establishing Free Schools in the County of Albermarle states: " The board may prescribe the methods of instruction and the books to be used, provided, That they shall not be immoral or irreligious in their tendency or of a sectarian character." (*Session Laws* 1848-9, Ch. 110, Sec. 9, Act March 14, 1849.) In an act of 1849 for the establishment of a Free School System in King George County we find: " No books of an immoral tendency and none of a strictly sectarian or partisan character shall be used therein." (*Session Laws* 1848-9, Ch. 113, Sec. 8, Act March 8, 1849.)

Washington: " Every board of directors unless otherwise especially provided by law, shall have power and it shall be their duty: . . . To exclude from schools and from school libraries, all books, papers, tracts or catechisms of an infidel, sectarian, or partisan character." (*Act* Nov. 28, 1883, Title IV, Ch. 38.) " No books, tracts, papers, catechisms or other publications of a partisan or denominational character shall be used or distributed in any school; . . . and any teacher who shall violate these provisions shall forfeit his permit or certificate for the period of one year." (*Act* Nov. 28, 1883, Title IX, Sec. 53.) " Every board of directors unless otherwise specially provided by law shall have power and it shall be their duty: . . . To exclude from schools and school libraries all books, tracts, papers and other publications of any immoral or pernicious tendency, or of a sectarian or partisan character." (Hill's *Annotated Statutes and Codes* 1891, Ch. V, Sec. 791, Act March 27, 1890.) The same provision is found in Ballinger's Annotated Codes and Statutes of 1897, Sec. 2311.[10]

Wisconsin: An act of 1883 relating to the adoption of and change in text-books provides: " But no text-books shall be permitted in any free public schools which would have a tendency to inculcate sectarian ideas." (*Session Laws* 1883, Ch. 251, Sec. 3, Act March 31, 1883.) " The board of education in any city shall determine what text-books shall be used in its schools, make a list of such books, file a copy with their clerk or secretary and keep a copy posted in each school building. But no text-books which would have a tendency to inculcate sectarian ideas shall be used in any public school." (*Statutes* 1898, Sec. 440a.)

To the second policy mentioned — that forbidding the exclusion of the Bible as a sectarian book and prescribing the method of its use, belong the following laws:

Dakota Territory: " No sectarian doctrine shall be taught or inculcated in any of the public schools of the corporation — but the Holy Scriptures without note or comment may be used therein." (*Session Laws* 1887, Ch. 47, Sec. 141, Schools in Cities, Towns and Villages.) " No sectarian doctrine shall be taught in any public school; but the Bible may be read in school not to exceed ten minutes daily, without sectarian comment; and no pupil shall be required to read it contrary to the wishes of his parent or guardian or other person having him in charge." (*Session Laws* 1887, Ch. 47, Sec. 19.)

Florida: " The reading of the Bible in, and short devotional exercises of a non-sectarian character at the opening of school, are not to be prohibited but no pupil is to be required to engage in them against his conscience, or contrary to the wishes of his parent or guardian." (*2nd Session* 1869, Act January 30, 1869,

Sec. 30.) Twenty years later in 1889 the clause excusing students who were opposed to reading the Bible was dropped from the law, which then read as follows: "The reading of the Bible in, and short devotional exercises of a non-sectarian character at the opening of the school are not to be prohibited." (*2nd Session* 1889, No. 26, Act June 8, 1889, Sec. 31.)

Georgia: "The county board of education shall prescribe, from time to time, what text-books and books of reference shall be used in the common schools of the county: Provided: that the Bible shall not be excluded from the common or public schools of the state. The county board shall not be permitted to introduce into the schools any text or miscellaneous books of a sectarian or sectional character. No teacher shall receive pay for any pupil who is allowed to use any other than the prescribed text-books." (*Code* 1895, Sec. 1365.)

Indiana: "The Bible shall not be excluded from the public schools of the state." (*Annotated Statutes Revision* 1894, Sec. 5980, Act Mar. 6, 1865.)

Iowa: "The Bible shall not be excluded from any school or institution in the state, nor shall any pupil be required to read it contrary to the wishes of his parent or guardian." (*Revised Statutes* 1873, Sec. 1764.) This is repeated in the Code of 1897, Sec. 2805.

Kansas: "No sectarian or religious doctrine shall be taught or inculcated in any of the public schools of the city; but nothing in this section shall be construed to prohibit the reading of the Holy Scriptures." (*General Statutes* 1905, Sec. 6816. Also *General Statutes* 1901, Sec. 6284, Act April 7, 1876. Cities of first class.) "No sectarian doctrine shall be taught or inculcated in any of the public schools of the city, but the Holy Scriptures without note or comment may be used therein." (*General Statutes* 1905, Sec. 6850; 1901, Sec. 6318; Act April 7, 1876. Cities of second class.)

Louisiana: "The Bible shall not be excluded from any school or institution in this state, under the control of the board, nor shall any pupil be required to read it, contrary to the wishes of his parent or guardian." (*Revised Statutes* 1870, Sec. 1288.)

Massachusetts: " The school committee shall require the daily reading of some portion of the Bible in the common English version; but shall never direct any school books calculated to favor the tenets of any particular sect of Christians to be purchased or used in any of the town schools." (*General Statutes* 1859, Ch. 38, Sec. 27, Acts 1855, Ch. 410.) " The school committee shall require the daily reading of some portion of the Bible, without written note or oral comment, in the public schools; but they shall require no scholar to read from any particular version, whose parent or guardian shall declare that he has conscientious scruples against allowing him to read therefrom, nor shall they ever direct any school books, calculated to favor the tenets of any particular sect of Christians, to be purchased or read in any of the public schools." (*General Laws* 1862, Ch. 57, Act March 6, 1862.) " The school committee shall require the daily reading in the public schools of some portion of the Bible, without written note or oral comment; but they shall not require a scholar whose parent or guardian informs the teacher in writing that he has conscientious scruples against it, to read from any particular version, or to take any personal part in the reading; nor shall they direct to be purchased or used in the public schools books calculated to favor the tenets of any particular sect of Christians." (*Public Statutes* 1882, Ch. 44, Sec. 32.) "A portion of the Bible shall be used daily in the public schools, without written note or oral comment; but a pupil whose parent or guardian informs the teacher in writing that he has conscientious scruples against it, shall not be required to read from any particular version, or to take any personal part in the reading. The school committee shall not purchase or use school books in the public schools calculated to favor the tenets of any particular religious sect." (*Revised Laws* 1901, Pt. 1, Title I., Ch. 42, Sec. 19.)

Mississippi: " Be it further enacted, That the Bible shall not be excluded from the schools of the state." (*Session Laws* 1870, Ch. 1, Sec. 50, Act July 4, 1870.) " Be it further enacted that the Bible shall not be excluded from the public free schools of this state." (*Session Laws* 1878, Act March 5, 1878, Sec. 43.)

New Jersey: " It shall not be lawful for any teacher, trustee or trustees to introduce into or have performed in any school receiving its proportion of public money, any religious service, ceremony or forms whatsoever, except reading the Bible and repeating the Lord's Prayer." (*General Statutes* 1895, Sec. 220, Act April 30, 1894, Ch. CII, Sess. of 1894.) " No religious service or exercise, except the reading of the Bible and the repeating of the Lord's Prayer shall be held in any school receiving any portion of the money appropriated for the support of public schools." (*Session Laws* 1900, Ch. 96, Art. VIII, Sec. 115.) This is repeated in *Session Laws* of 1902, Ch. 36, Art. VIII, Sec. 108 and *School Laws* of 1908, p. 51, Sec. 114.

New York: " But no school shall be entitled to a portion of the school moneys, in which the religious, sectarian doctrine or tenet of any particular Christian or other religious sect shall be taught, inculcated or practiced, or in which any book or books containing compositions favorable or prejudicial to the particular doctrine or tenets of any Christian sect, or which shall teach the doctrine or tenets of any other religious sect, or which shall refuse to permit the visits and examination provided for in this act." (Laws of *67th Session,* Ch. 320, Act May 7, 1844.) The above is repeated in the Revised Statutes of 1846, Pt. 1, Ch. XV, Sec. 208, in the Laws of the 74th Session, Ch. 386, Sec. 18, Act of July 3, 1851, and in the Act of July 1, 1882, and applies to New York City. By the act of May 7, 1844, it was also made the duty of the county superintendent of schools to examine and ascertain, and report to the board of education of New York City whether any of the provisions of the act in relation to religious sectarian teaching and books had been violated in any of the different wards of the city. (Laws of *67th Session,* Ch. 320, Sec. 44, Act May 7, 1844.) The foregoing was repeated in the Laws of the 74th Session, Ch. 386, Sec. 11, Act of July 3, 1851.

By this same act of May 7, 1844, it was made the duty of the commissioners, inspectors and trustees in each ward, from time to time and as frequently as need be, to examine, ascertain and report to the board of education of the City of New York whether the provisions in relation to the teaching of sectarian doctrine or the use of sectarian books had been violated.

(Laws of *67th Session,* Ch. 320, Sec. 13, Act May 7, 1844.) The foregoing was repeated in the Revised Statutes of 1846, Pt. 1, Ch. XV, Sec. 209. In 1882 the duty was imposed upon the inspectors or a majority of them only. (*Act* July 1, 1882.)

The same law of May 7, 1844 contained the following: " But nothing herein contained shall authorize the board of education (New York City) to exclude the Holy Scriptures without note or comment, or any selections therefrom, from any of the schools provided for by this act; but it shall not be competent for said board of education to decide what version, if any, of the Holy Scriptures without note or comment, shall be used in any of the said schools; provided, that nothing herein contained shall be so construed as to violate the rights of conscience as secured by the constitution of this state and the United States." (Laws of *67th Session,* Ch. 320, Sec. 12, Act May 7, 1844.) The same provision was repeated in the Revised Statutes of 1846, Pt. 1, Ch. XV, Sec. 208; in the Laws of the 74th Session, Ch. 386, Sec. 18, Act of July 3, 1851; and in Act of July 1, 1882, Ch. 410, Sec. 1062.

In 1850 the following was enacted with regard to the schools of Brooklyn: " No school in said city shall be entitled to any portion of the school moneys, in which the religious, sectarian doctrine or tenets of any particular Christian or other religious sect shall be taught or inculcated, or which shall refuse or prohibit visits or examinations by the city superintendent or members of the board of education of said city; provided, that this section shall not be deemed to prohibit the use of the Holy Scriptures without note or comment." (Laws of *73rd Session,* Ch. 143, Sec. 19, Act April 4, 1850.)

North Dakota: " The Bible shall not be deemed a sectarian book. It shall not be excluded from any public school. It may at the option of the teacher be read in school without sectarian comment, not to exceed ten minutes daily. No pupil shall be required to read it nor be present in the schoolroom during the reading thereof contrary to the wishes of his parents or guardian or other person having him in charge." (*Political Code* 1899, Sec. 754, Laws of 1890, Ch. 62, Sec. 134.)

Oklahoma: " No sectarian doctrine shall be taught or inculcated in any of the public schools of the city; but the Holy Scriptures, without note or comment, may be read therein at the discretion of each teacher." (*Revised and Annotated Statutes* 1903, Ch. 77, Art. 9, Sec. 6267. Applying to cities of the first class.) By the act of Feb. 19, 1895, the same provision was made to apply to public schools in union school districts. (*Revised and Annotated Statutes* 1903, Ch. 77, Art. 8, Sec. 6247, Act Feb. 19, 1895.) " No sectarian or religious doctrine shall be taught or inculcated in any of the public schools in this territory, but nothing in this section shall be construed to prohibit the reading of the Holy Scriptures." (*Revised and Annotated Statutes* 1903, Ch. 77, Art. 3, Sec. 6189.) In the School Laws of 1908 the above section remains the same with the substitution of " state " for " territory."

South Dakota: In an act entitled " Cities, Towns, and Adjacent Territory, Organized as Independent Districts " we find: " No sectarian doctrine may be taught or inculcated in any of the schools of the corporation; but the Bible, without sectarian comment may be read therein." (*Political Code* 1903, Sec. 2423.)

West Virginia: "All teachers employed in the public schools of this state shall read or cause to be read at least one chapter from the Bible, in a language understood by the scholars, every day at the opening of the school; inculcate the duties of piety, morality and respect for the laws and government of their country." (*Session Laws* 1866, Ch. 74, Sec. 29, Act February 26, 1866.)

CHAPTER VIII

LAWS FORBIDDING THE ESTABLISHMENT OF RELIGIOUS TESTS

The elimination of ecclesiastical or sectarian control or influence from public education has been sought in many states through laws forbidding the setting up of any particular religious belief or affiliation with any particular religious sect as a necessary qualification for or bar to, membership on boards of trustees, positions as school administrators or instructors, or the right to attend public schools as students. Sometimes the law has gone so far as to prevent even private schools which have enjoyed the privileges of incorporation from setting up such tests.

Alabama: We find the following in the Code of 1852 relating to the University of Alabama: "No religious qualification or test must be required from any student, trustee, president, professor, or other officer of such university, or as a condition for admission to any privilege therein." (*Code* 1852, Title 11, Ch. II, Par. 850.)

Arizona: The Revised Statutes of 1901 contain the following with regard to the territorial university: "Nor shall any sectarian tenets or opinions be required to entitle any person to be admitted as a student in said university; and no such tenets or opinions shall be required as a qualification for any person as a regent, tutor, or professor of such university." (*Revised Statutes* 1901, Par. 3638.)

Georgia: With regard to the state university we find the following enactments: "The trustees shall not exclude any person of any religious denomination whatsoever from free and equal liberty and advantages of education, or from any of the liberties, privileges and immunities of the university in his education, on account of his, her or their speculative sentiments in religion, or being of a different religious profession." (*Act*

82

Jan. 27, 1785, Sec. 11.) "All officers elected or appointed for the university shall be of the Christian religion, but no person of any religious denomination shall be excluded from equal advantages of education and the immunities of the university on account of their speculative sentiments in religion or being of a different religious profession from the trustees or faculty." (*Code* 1861, Sec. 1127.) A radical step toward secularization is seen in an act of 1877: " Be it enacted by the General Assembly of the state of Georgia and it is hereby enacted by the authority of the same: That section 1203 of the Code of Georgia be amended by striking out the words, — ' all officers elected or appointed for the University of Georgia shall be of the Christian religion.'" (*Session Laws* 1877, No. XII, Act Feb. 26, 1877.) This same act of 1877 also released the chancellor of the university, its professors and tutors from taking certain religious oaths prescribed in the charter of the university. (*Act* Feb. 26, 1877, Sec. 17.) This is repeated in the Code of 1895, Sec. 1293. Freedom of religious belief on the part of students at the university is assured successively by the Act of 1785 quoted above and by the Law of 1877 in these words: " No person of any religious denomination shall be excluded from equal advantages of education and the immunities of the university on account of their speculative sentiments in religion, or being of a different religious profession from the trustees or faculty." (*Act* Feb. 26, 1877.) This last provision is continued in the Code of 1895, Sec. 1292.

Idaho: With regard to the Albion State Normal School we find the following: " No religious or sectarian tests shall be applied in the selection of teachers, and none shall be adopted in said school." (*School Laws* 1903, p. 17, Sec. 37.) This same provision is found with regard to the Academy of Idaho (*School Laws* 1903, p. 20, Sec. 51), and the Lewiston State Normal School (*School Laws* 1905, p. 9, Sec. 961.) With regard to the State University the law reads: " No sectarian or partisan test shall ever be allowed or exercised in the appointment of regents or in the election of professors, teachers or other officers of the university or in the admission of students thereto or for any purpose whatever." (*School Laws* 1907, p 10, Sec. 934.)

Illinois: In the legislation of this state we find a number of illustrations of the practice of forbidding the setting up of religious tests in schools enjoying the privilege of incorporation. In an act incorporating Alton Female Institute it is provided that no particular religious faith shall be required of those who become trustees of the institution. (*Act* Jan. 9, 1835, Sec. 2.) An act incorporating Bloomington Female Seminary of Learning provided that said institution and its preparatory department should be open to all denominations of Christians, and the profession of any particular religious faith should not be required of those who became students. (*Act* Jan. 9, 1836, Sec. 9.) An act to incorporate Danville Academy provided that no particular religious faith should be required of those who should become trustees, students, teachers, officers, or servants of said institution. (*Act* Jan. 15, 1836, Sec. 3.) An act incorporating Burst Prairie Manual Labor Seminary provided that said institution should be open to all denominations of Christians, and the profession of any particular religious faith should not be required of those who became students. (*Act* Jan. 15, 1836, Sec. 6.) Similar provisions are to be found in the acts incorporating Mt. Carmel Academy (*Act* Jan. 16, 1836, Sec. 5), Carmi Academy (*Act* Jan. 16, 1836, Sec. 7), Franklin Manual Labor College (*Act* Jan. 18, 1836, Sec. 4), Fayette County Manual Labor Seminary (*Act* July 11, 1837, Sec. 6), and Hamilton Primary School (*Act* Feb. 1, 1840.)

Indiana: Concerning the State University we find the following: " No religious qualification shall be required for any student, trustee, president, professor or other officer of such university, or as a condition for admission to any privilege in the same." (*Annotated Statutes Revision* 1894, Sec. 6071, Act May 6, 1853.)

Iowa: An act of 1842 incorporating Mt. Pleasant Institute provided that said institution should be under the charge of the Methodist Episcopal Church but there should be no religious test for the admission of students. (*Act* Feb. 17, 1842, Sec. 9.) A former act of incorporation did not contain this provision. (*Act* Jan. 23, 1839.) An act incorporating Iowa City College under the control of the Methodist Episcopal Church specified that it was to be conducted on the most liberal principles, should be accessible to all religious denominations, and that it was designed for the benefit of "our citizens in general." The youth of every class of citizens and of every religious denomination were to be freely admitted to equal advantages and privileges of education. (*Act* Feb. 15, 1843, preamble and Sec. 1.) Mt. Pleasant Institute, incorporated by an act of Feb. 15, 1844, became by an act of 1855, Iowa Wesleyan University. This act of 1855 provided that "said university shall be forever open on equal terms to all who may wish to avail themselves of its advantages, irrespective of religious opinion." (*Act* Jan. 25, 1855, Sec. 12.)

Kentucky: Regarding its Agricultural and Mechanical College we find the following: "In the appointment of presidents, professors, or instructors no preference shall be shown to any religious denomination." (*Statutes* 1903, Ch. 3, Sec. 19.)

Louisiana: Referring to the board of regents of the State University we find the following: "They shall not make the religious tenet of any person a condition of admission to any privilege or office in the university." (*Acts* 1855, No. 320, Sec. 8.) This is repeated in the Revised Statutes of 1870, Sec. 1358.

Massachusetts: "No person shall be excluded from a public school on account of race, color or religious opinion of the applicant or scholar." (*General Statutes* 1859, Ch. 41, Sec. 9.) This is repeated in Public Statutes of 1882, Ch. 48, Sec. 10. In the Revised Laws of 1901 we find: "No child shall be excluded from a public school of any city or town on account of race, color or religion." (*Revised Laws* 1901, Pt. I, Title I, Ch. 44, Sec. 3.)

Michigan: An act of 1837 changing the name of Michigan and Huron Institute to Kalamazoo Literary Institute, states: "Said institute and departments shall be open to all Christian denominations and the profession of any religious faith shall not be required of those who become students." (*Act* March 21, 1837, Sec. 5.) In 1855 there was passed a law providing the terms on which colleges, academies and other institutions of learning might be incorporated. This provided that no religious test whatever should be required of any pupil in such institutions. (*Session Laws* 1855, Act Feb. 9, 1855, Sec. 6.)

Minnesota: " In the selection of professors, instructors, officers, and assistants of the university, in the studies and exercises, and in the management and government thereof, no partiality or preference shall be shown on account of political or religious beliefs or religion." (*School Laws* 1907, p. 130, Sec. 322.)

Missouri: An act of 1825 providing for the management and protection of school lands and the establishment and government of public schools reads: "And in the choice of visitors, instructors and pupils, no preference shall ever be given on account of religious opinions; nor shall any ordinance, by-law, or regulation ever be made in any wise to control or interfere with the rights of conscience, or belief on the subject of religion, or the free exercise of religious worship." (*Act* Jan. 17, 1825, Sec. 29.) An act of 1835 for the establishment of public schools contains a similar provision. (*Act* March 19, 1835, Sec. 35.) An act of 1840 incorporating Polk County Academy provides: " No preference shall be given nor discrimination made on account of religious opinion nor shall any by-law be enacted that will, or may, in any wise control or interfere with the exercise of conscience, or the free exercise of religious worship." (*Act* Dec. 12, 1840, Sec. 7.) An act of 1841 incorporating Union Academy reads: " Provided, no preference shall be given or discrimination be made in the choice of trustees, professors, teachers or students, on account of religious opinions, or the exercise of religious worship." (*Act* Jan. 2, 1841, Sec. 5.) An act of 1845, incorporating an Academy in the town of Perryville, specifies that " No trustee, professor, or teacher, shall at any time make or enact any by-laws, ordinance, rules, or regulations that will or may in any wise control or interfere with the right of free exercise of religious worship." (*Act* Feb. 25, 1845, Sec. 7.) An act of 1845 incorporating Liberty Institute reads as follows: " No preference shall be given, or any discrimination made in the choice of trustees, or other officers or students, on account of religious sentiments or the want of them; nor shall the trustees make any by-laws, or other regulations that may interfere with the rights of conscience, the free exercise of religious worship or the enjoyment of innocent amusements." (*Act* March 15, 1845, Sec. 7.) An act of the same date as the above incorporating an academy in the town of St. Ferdinand contains the following:

" In the choice of trustees, professors, teachers, and students, no preference, distinction or discrimination shall be made on account of religious opinions or professions of faith, nor shall the trustees at any time make any by-laws, ordinances or regulations that may in any wise control or interfere with the rights of conscience or the exercise of religious worship." (*Act* March 15, 1845, Sec. 10.)

Montana: With regard to the State University the following was enacted in 1893: " The state board of education shall have power to determine the moral and educational qualifications of applicants for admission to the various courses of instruction; but no sectarian or partisan test shall ever be allowed or exercised in the appointment of professors, instructors, officers or employees of the university, or in the admission of students thereto, or for any purpose whatever." (*Political Code* 1895, Sec. 1545, Act Feb. 17, 1893.)

Nebraska: An act of 1857 incorporating Brownville College provides that said college and its preparatory and other departments shall be open to all denominations of Christians; and the profession of any particular religious faith shall not be required of those who become students. (*Act* Feb. 9, 1857, Sec. 12.) Similar provisions are found in acts incorporating Dakota City Collegiate and Preparatory Institute (*Act* Feb. 12, 1857), Oneida College (*Session Laws* 1857, p. 212, Sec. 14), and St. John's University (*Act* Feb. 13, 1857). An act of 1871 supplementary to an Act of June 20, 1867, entitled, "An Act to Locate, Establish and Endow a State Normal School " provides as follows: " No religious or sectarian test shall ever be applied in the selection of teachers, and none shall be adopted in the school." (*Session Laws* 1870-71, Act March 3, 1871, Sec. 10.) This provision is repeated in the Session Laws of 1881, Sub-Division XIII, Sec. 9, Act of March 1, 1881, and in the Laws of 1907, Sec. 5579.

New Jersey: One of the earliest instances of the enactment of a provision forbidding the establishment of religious tests in education is found in the charter granted by the royal government of New Jersey in 1746 to the College of New Jersey. It provided that no person of any religious denomination whatsoever should be excluded from the free and equal liberty and advantages of education, or from any of the liberties, privileges, or immunities of the said college, on account of his or their being of a religious profession different from the said trustees of the said college.[1]   An act of 1881 provides as follows: " No child between the ages of five and eighteen years shall be excluded from any public school in this state on account of his or her religion, nationality or color.   Any member of a board of district trustees or member of a board of education excluding any such child on such grounds is declared guilty of a misdemeanor." (*General Statutes* 1895, Sec. 131, p. 3036, Act March 23, 1881, Sec. 1 and 2.)   By a later law the age limits in the above were changed to four to twenty years.   (*Session Laws* 1900, Ch. 96, Art. IX, Sec. 126.)   This provision was repeated in the Session Laws of 1902, Ch. 36, Art. IV, Sec. 119, and in the Session Laws of 1903 (Special Session), Ch. 1, Art. IX, Sec. 125.

New York: The charter granted to Kings College by George II, in 1754, forbids the governors of the college to make any laws " to exclude any person of any religious denomination whatever from equal liberty and advantage of education, or from any of the degrees, liberties, privileges, benefits, or immunities of the said college, on account of his particular tenets in matters of religion." (*Charters, Acts and Official Documents,* pp. 10-24, compiled by John B. Pine, New York, 1895.)   By an act of 1784 it was specified that the president of Columbia University was henceforth to be elected from among the professors of the several colleges of the universities, and no professor should be accounted in any wise ineligible because of any religious tenet or tenets that he might or should possess, or be compelled to take any religious test oath.   (*Act* May 1, 1784, Ch. 51.)   An act of 1787 reads: " No president or professor shall be ineligible for or by reason of any religious tenet or tenets that he may or shall possess." (*Act* April 13, 1787, Ch. LXXXII, Sec. 20.)   This was repeated in the act of April 5, 1813, Ch. LIX.   An act of 1826 changing the name of the Free School Society of New York City to the Public School Society of New York City states its purpose to be to educate all children, whether the proper objects of gratuitous education or not, and without regard to the

---

[1] Given in the History of the College of New Jersey, 1, 90-7. John McLean, Philadelphia, 1877.

religious sects to which they or their parents might belong. (*Act* Jan. 28, 1826.) The Revised Statutes of 1846 contain the following: " No religious qualification or test shall be required from any trustee, president, principal or other officer of any incorporated college or academy or as a condition for admission to any privilege in the same." (*Revised Statutes* 1846, Ch. XV, Tit. 1, Art. 5, Sec. 64.)

North Dakota: An act of 1883 contains the following with regard to the university: " No sectarian or partisan test shall ever be allowed or exercised in the appointment of trustees or in the election of professors, teachers, or other officers of the university or in the admission of students thereto or for any purpose whatever." (*Political Code* 1899, Sec. 881, Acts 1883, Ch. 40, Sec. 5.)

Oklahoma: With regard to the University of Oklahoma we find the following legislation: " No sectarian or partisan test shall ever be allowed or exercised in the appointment of regents or in the election of professors or other officers of the university, or in the admission of students thereto, or for any purpose whatever." (*Revised and Annotated Statutes* 1903, Ch. 77, Art. 17, Sec. 6384, Act Dec. 19, 1890.) With regard to the Normal School at Edmond we find: " The board of education in their regulations and the principal in his supervision and government of the school shall exercise a watchful guardianship over the morals of the pupils at all times during their attendance on the same, but no religious or sectarian tests shall be applied in the selection of teachers, and none shall be adopted in the school." (*Revised and Annotated Statutes* 1903, Ch. 77, Art. 19, Sec. 6450, Act Dec. 25, 1890.) An act of 1897 relating to the Colored Agricultural and Normal University contains the same provision. (*Revised and Annotated Statutes* 1903, Ch. 77, Art. 23, Sec. 6503, Act Mar. 12, 1897.)

Oregon: " No political or sectarian test shall ever be allowed or applied in the appointment of regents, professors, teachers, or employees of the university, nor shall the majority of the regents be, at any one time, members of any one religious denomination or be appointed from or reside in any one county of the state." (*Codes and Statutes* 1902, Tit. XXXIII, Ch. VI, Sec. 3119. Also *Session Laws* 1876, p. 57, Sec. 11.)

South Carolina: An act to establish and provide for the support of a state normal school provides: "No religious test shall be required of any one connected with the state normal school," etc. (*Session Laws* 1872-3, No. 333, Sec. 10.) The Revised Statutes of 1873 contain the following with regard to the University of South Carolina: "Neither the said board of trustees nor the faculty of the university shall make any distinction in the admission of students or the management of the university on account of race, color, or creed." (*Revised Statutes* 1873, Ch. XLII, Sec. 34.)

South Dakota: The Political Code of 1903 contains the following with regard to state normal schools: "The board of regents in their regulations and the principals in their supervision and the government of the schools shall exercise a watchful guardianship over the morals of the pupils at all times during their attendance at the same, but no religious or sectarian tests shall be applied in the seletcion of teachers and none shall be adopted in the schools." (*Political Code* 1903, Sec. 603.)

Texas: Under the republic the following laws were enacted: "An act incorporating the trustees of Washington College in which it was provided that, the privileges, benefits, and facilities of the said college should be equally accessible to all without regard to peculiarity of opinion." (*Act* June 5, 1837, Sec. 7.) "An act to establish and incorporate the College of Decalb, in which it was made the duty of the trustees to 'take effectual care that students of all religious denominations may and shall be admitted to equal advantages, and that they receive alike fair and generous treatment during their residence thereat.'" (*Act* Jan. 26, 1839, Sec. 5.) The act of 1881 by which the University of the state of Texas was established provided as follows: "No religious qualifications shall be required for admission to any office or privilege in the university." (*Session Laws* 1881, Ch. 75, Act March 30, 1881, Sec. 20.) The same provision is found in the Revised Statutes of 1895, Art. 3853.

Virginia: An act of 1839 incorporating Emory and Henry College declares that no person "shall be ineligible to any office or trust appertaining to the college, or be excluded from a full and free participation in the privileges and benefits of the college on account of his religious tenets." (*Session Laws* 1839, Ch. 184, Act March 25, 1839.) An act of 1842 incorporating Green Bank Academy and the Trustees of Northwestern Academy provided, with regard to the latter, that no person should be ineligible to any office or trust appertaining to the academy, or be excluded from a full and free participation in the privileges and benefits of the academy on account of his religious tenets. (*Session Laws* 1841-2, Ch. 147, Sec. 8, Act March 26, 1842.)

Washington: An act of 1890 concerning the Normal School at Cheney states: " The board of trustees in their regulations and the principal in his supervision and government of the school shall exercise a watchful guardianship over the morals of the pupils at all times during their attendance upon the same, but no religious or sectarian tests shall be applied in the selection of teachers, and none shall be adopted in the school." (Hill's *Annotated Statutes and Codes* 1891, Tit. X, Ch. XVI, Sec. 922, Act March 22, 1890, Sec. 17.)

Wisconsin: An act passed in 1857 for the encouragement of academies and normal schools provides that the income from twenty-five per cent of the gross proceeds arising from the sale of swamp and overflowed lands granted by Congress to Wisconsin shall be distributed to such normal schools and academies and in such ratio as the Board of Regents shall designate, and no religious test shall ever be required of any student or scholar in any of the institutions or schools receiving any of the said funds. (*Session Laws* 1857, p. 93, Act March 7, 1857.) An act of 1858 providing for the incorporation of academies and other institutions of learning states that no religious test or qualification shall ever be required of any trustees, officer, teacher, or pupil therein. (*Session Laws* 1858, p. 53, Act April 21, 1858.) An act incorporating Jefferson Liberal Institute runs as fol- lows: " No religious tenets or opinions shall be requisite to entitle any person to be admitted as a student in such institute, and no such tenets or opinions shall be required as a qualification for any professor, tutor, or teacher of said institute; and no student of said institute shall be required to attend religious wor- ship in any particular denomination." (*Private and Local Laws, Session* 1866, Ch. 516, Sec. 10, Act April 12, 1866.) An act of the same year incorporating Prairie de Chien College provides: "No tests of a political or religious character shall be required of any professor, teacher, or student in the institution." (*Private and Local Laws, Session* 1866, Ch. 513, Sec. 5, Act April 12, 1866.)   An act of 1880 amending an act of 1854 incorporating a German and English Academy in Milwaukee provide that no religious test shall be required of the teachers or scholars of said school.   (*Session Laws* 1880, Ch. 61, Sec. 1, Act Feb. 28, 1880.)   The Statutes of 1898 contain the following with regard to the state university: "No sectarian or partisan tests sh ever be allowed or exercised in the appointment of regents or in the election of professors, teachers, or other officers of the university, or in the admission of students thereto or for any purpose whatever." (*Statutes* 1898, Sec. 381.)

Wyoming: The following was enacted regarding the territorial university in 1886: "No religious qualification or test shall be required of any student, trustee, president, professor, tutor, or officer of such university or as a condition for admission for any privileges of the same." (*Session Laws* 1886, Ch. 37, Sec. 45.)   An act of 1890 contains the following: "In the employment of teachers in the public schools in this state, no discrimination shall be made in the question of pay on account of sex, nor on acount of the religious belief of the applicant for the position of teacher when the persons are equally qualified and the labor is the same." (*Revised Statutes* 1899, Sec. 64. *Session Laws* 1890-91, Ch. 21, Act Dec. 31, 1890.)   Regarding the Wyoming Agricultural College we find: "No religious qualification or test shall be required of any student, trustee, president, professor, tutor, or officer of said institution or as a condition for admission to any privilege in the same," etc.   (*Revised Statutes* 1899, Sec. 513.   *Session Laws* 1890-91, Ch. 92, Sec. 11, Act June 10, 1891.)   Regarding the university there is the following: "No sectarian or partisan test shall ever be exercised or allowed in the appointment of trustees, or in the election or removal of professors, teachers, or other officers of the university, or in the admission of students thereto, or for any purpose whatsoever." (*Revised Statutes* 1899, Sec. 491.   *Session Laws* 1890-91, Ch. 75, Sec. 6, Act Jan. 10, 1891.)

CHAPTER IX

LAWS FORBIDDING THE APPROPRIATION OF PUBLIC FUNDS TO SCHOOLS UNDER ECCLESIASTICAL CONTROL

In our early history it was a common practice, as we have already shown in Chapter IV, for states to contribute funds to schools entirely or in part under church control. At times these grants were unconditional; at other times they were given with the understanding that a certain number of indigent children were to be educated free of tuition charges; again the conditions of the grants were that the schools assisted should make certain reports to the state authorities or submit to inspection thereby.

With the establishment of large school funds derived chiefly from the sale of public land, and with the increased revenues derived from taxation, the question of the proper disposal of this state aid became an important one. The vision of universal education, the logical corollary of universal manhood suffrage, began to be caught sight of by more and more of our leaders. The increasing revenues from funds and taxation made the realization of this vision seem more and more a possibility. But with the increasing religious heterogeneity of our population centers the problem of an equitable distribution of these funds began to be increasingly difficult of solution. To grant funds to one denomination for supporting schools meant that funds must be granted to all denominations that chose to establish schools and apply for help. Those who had dreamed of universal education supported by state funds saw that there was great danger of the realization of their dream being frustrated through the frittering away of these funds among a horde of petty denominational schools. Economy demanded concentration. Moreover, schools directly controlled by the state could be much more easily maintained at any given standard the state might desire than schools controlled by any ecclesiastical power. There was, too, an increasing number of those who either claimed no church affiliation or else found too few of like faith with themselves in certain communities to think of carrying on schools. For these, if education was to be universal, the state must provide schools. So in the interest of economy, in order that the state funds might be used to the greatest advantage in the effort to bring about universal education, it was necessary that state support should be limited to schools controlled by the state. We find therefore in the legislation of a considerable number of states laws forbidding the use of public school funds, sometimes the use of any public funds, for the support of schools controlled by the church, or, to use the more general term, for the support of schools in which the control of the state is not absolute.

Alabama: An act of the Alabama legislature passed in 1854 for the regulation of a system of public schools in Mobile provided: "The whole revenue arising to said board (Board of School Commissioners of Mobile) shall be employed as a common fund for the instruction of the youth of said county; no portion thereof shall be diverted to the maintenance or support of any school that is not strictly common to all children of the county or to any that is under sectarian influence or control." (*Session Laws* 1853-54, No. 307, Act. Jan. 16, 1854.)

Arizona: An act of the Arizona legislature passed in 1883 contained the following: ". . . nor shall any school whatever under the control of any religious denomination or which has not been taught in accordance with the provision of this act, receive any of the public school funds." (*Session Laws 12th Session* 1883, No. 33. Sec. 62.) In addition to the above the revision of 1895 contains this provision: ". . . and upon satisfactory evidence of such violation the county school superintendent must withhold all apportionment of school moneys from said school." (*Revision* 1895, Ch. XI, Sec. 88.)

California: In 1855 the legislature of California enacted the following with regard to the Establishment, Support and Regulation of Common Schools in Incorporated Cities and Towns: "The common council on petition of fifty heads of white families, citizens of the district, shall establish a school or schools in said district and shall award said school or schools a pro rata of the school fund, provided . . . and said schools so established shall be under the supervision and control of the common council as are all other common schools within their jurisdiction, under the provisions of this act." (*Session Laws* 1855, Ch. CLXXXV. Act May 3, 1855, Sec. 22.)

Illinois: The following detailed and complete prohibition of the donation of public funds to church-controlled schools was enacted by the Illinois legislature in 1872: " No county, city, town, township, school district, or other public corporation shall ever make any appropriation or pay from any school fund whatever, anything in aid of any sectarian purpose, or to help support or sustain any school, academy, seminary, college, university, or other literary or scientific institution, controlled by any church or sectarian denomination whatever; nor shall any grant or donation of money or other personal property ever be made by any such corporation to any church or for any sectarian purpose." (*Act* July 1, 1872, Sec. 77.)

Iowa: An act of the Iowa legislature in 1847 providing for the establishment of a state university at Iowa City, contained the following provision which was repeated in an act of 1858: " Said university shall never be under the exclusive control of any religious denomination whatever." (*Act* Feb. 25, 1847, Sec 10, and *Act* Mar. 12, 1858, Sec. 79.) In 1872 an act was passed containing the following: " No appropriation of public money or other property shall be made, and no gift, loan or appropriation of money or property shall be authorized or made by the corporate authorities, supervisors, or trustees of any county, township, city, or town, or municipal organiation of this state, to or in favor of, any institution, school or association or object, which is under ecclesiastical or sectarian management or control." (*Act* April 17, 1872.)

Louisiana: The legislature of Louisiana in 1855 enacted the following with regard to the State University: " The board of trustees shall not permit the seminary to be subject to the control of any religious denomination." (*Act* 1855, No. 317, Sec. 14.) In 1894 the following was enacted with regard to the parochial school boards of the state: "The parish boards of directors of the several parishes of this state are prohibited from entering into any contract, agreement, understanding or combination, tacitly or expressly, directly or indirectly, with any church, monastic or other religious order or association of any religious sect or denomination whatsoever, or with the representatives thereof, for the purpose of running or to defray the expenses for the running of any public school or schools of this state, together or in connection or in combination with any private or parochial school or other institution of learning which may be under the control, authority, supervision, administration, or management of any church, monastic or other religious order or association of any religious sect or denomination whatsoever." (*Acts* 1894, No. 52, Sec. 14.) Practically the same provisions are contained in an act of 1902. (*Act* No. 214, Session of 1902.)

Michigan: An act of the Michigan legislature reads as follows: "No school district shall apply any of the money received by it from the primary school interest fund, or from any and all other sources, for the support and maintenance of any school of a sectarian character, whether the same be under the control of any religious society, or made sectarian by the school district board." (*Compiled Laws* 1897, Par. 4676.)

Nevada: "No portion of the public school funds nor of money raised by state tax or specially appropriated for the support of public schools shall be devoted to any other object or purpose; nor shall any portion of the public school funds nor of money raised by state tax for the support of public schools, be in any way segregated, divided, or set apart for the use or benefit of any sectarian or secular society or association." (*General Statutes* 1885, Sec. 1332. Also *Compiled Laws* 1900, Sec. 1713.)

New Jersey: The legislature of New Jersey enacted a provision in 1881 providing that no portion of the public school funds should be used for the support of sectarian schools. (*General Statutes* 1895, Sec. 129, Act Mar. 16, 1881.)

New York: An act of the legislature of New York in 1871 providing for the local government of the City of New York declared: "It shall not be lawful for the mayor, aldermen, and commonalty of the city of New York or the board of supervisors of the county of New York, or the board of apportionment herein created, to appropriate or apply any portion of the tax herein authorized to be raised, in aid of any private or sectarian school or to any institution or enterprise that is under the control of any religious denomination, or to borrow any money on the faith or credit of the city to be applied to any such purpose . . ." (The foregoing not to apply however to a long list of charitable institutions.) (*94th Session,* Ch. 583; Act April 19, 1871, Sec. 6.) An act of 1882 provides that no money belonging to the city, or city and county of New York raised by taxation upon the property of the citizens thereof shall be appropriated in aid of any religious or denominational school. It likewise prohibits the sale of public property to such schools except at public auction to the highest bidder, and prohibits leasing city property to any such school except upon such terms as city property may be leased to private parties after the same has been duly advertised. (*105th Session,* Ch. 410, Act July 1, 1882.)

North Dakota: The legislature of North Dakota provided in 1891 that the state normal schools should be free from sectarian control. (*Laws* 1891, Ch. 89, Sec. 13, also *Pol. Code* 1899, Sec. 913.)

Texas: In 1884 the legislature of Texas declared that no part of the public school fund should be appropriated to or used for the support of any sectarian school. (*Laws Special Session* 1884, Ch. 25, Act Feb. 1884.)

Washington: The legislature of Washington enacted the following with regard to the State University in 1890: "The university shall never be under the control of any religious or sectarian denomination or society whatever." (Hill's *Annotated Statutes and Codes,* 1891, Title X, Ch. XVII, Sec. 947, Act March 27, 1890, Sec. 5.) The same act provided that all schools maintained or supported wholly or in part by the public funds should be forever free from sectarian control or influence. (Hill's *Annotated Statutes and Codes* 1891, Title X, Ch. IX, Sec. 816, Act March 27, 1890.)

CHAPTER X

CONSTITUTIONAL PROVISIONS CONCERNING THE AIM OF EDUCATION

Not only our laws, but our state constitutions as well, frequently contain provisions in which the aim of education is definitely set forth. All of the constitutions in force to-day, as well as a number that have been superseded, contain provisions for public instruction. It is in connection with these provisions, frequently as prefaces thereto, that we find these statements as to the purpose of the state in establishing schools. As with the laws enacted since the beginning of the national period, the provisions in which religion is mentioned as an aim of education are relatively few, while in almost all, the civic, professional, or industrial aims are emphasied. Knowledge, morality, virtue are recognized as essentials of good citizenship, and it is assumed to be the function of the school to impart the same, but little is heard of religion or the service of the church in this connection.

The following citations from various state constitutions set forth religion as one of the aims of education.

Massachusetts: ". . . and whereas the encouragement of arts and sciences, and all good literature, tends to the honor of God, the advantage of the Christian religion and the great benefit of this and the other United States of America," the powers, authorities, rights, privileges, etc., of the president and fellows of Harvard College are ratified and confirmed unto them and to their successors forever." (*Constitution* 1780, Part II, Ch. V, Sec. I, Art. I.)

Michigan: "Religion, morality, and knowledge being necessary to good government and the happiness of mankind, schools and the means of education shall forever be encouraged." (*Constitution* 1909, Art. XI, Sec. 1.)

98

Mississippi: "Religion, morality, and knowledge being necessary to good government, the preservation of liberty, and the happiness of mankind, schools and the means of education shall forever be encouraged in this state." (*Constitution* 1817, Art. VI, Sec. 16, and *Constitution* 1832, Art. VII, Sec. 14.)

North Carolina: "Religion, morality, and knowledge being necessary to good government and the happiness of mankind, schools and the means of education shall forever be encouraged." (*Constitutions* 1868 and 1876, Art. IX, Sec. 1.)

Ohio: ". . . But religion, morality, and knowledge being essentially necessary to the good government and the happiness of mankind, schools and the means of instruction shall forever be encouraged by legislative provision, not inconsistent with the rights of conscience." (*Constitution* 1802, Art. VII, Sec. 3.) Article I, Section VII, Bill of Rights of the Constitution of 1851, contains practically the same.

In the following citations from state constitutions the aim of education is set forth without any reference to religion.

Arkansas: "Knowledge and learning generally diffused through a community, being essential to the preservation of a free government . . . and diffusing the opportunities and advantages of education through the various parts of the state being highly conducive to this end . . . it shall be the duty of the general assembly to provide by law for the improvement of such lands as are or may hereafter be granted by the United States to this state for the use of schools." (*Constitution* 1836, Art. VII, Sec. 1.) "Knowledge and learning generally diffused throughout the community being essential to the preservation of a free government, and diffusing the opportunities and advantages of education through the various parts of the state being highly conducive to this end, it shall be the duty of the general assembly to provide by law for the improvement of such lands as are or hereafter may be granted by the United States to this state for the use of schools, and to apply any funds which may be raised from such lands or from any other source, to the accomplishment of the object for which they are or may be intended. The general assembly shall from time to time pass such laws as shall be calculated to encourage intellectual, scientific, and agricultural improvement . . . and countenance and encourage the principles of humanity, industry, and morality." (*Constitution* 1864, Art. VIII, Sec. 1.) "A general diffusion of knowledge and intelligence among all classes being essential to the preservation of the rights and liberties of the people; the general assembly shall establish and maintain a system of free schools," etc. (*Constitution* 1868, Art. IX, Sec. 1.) "Intelligence and virtue being the safeguards of liberty and the bulwark of a free and good government, the state shall ever maintain a general, suitable and efficient system of free schools," etc. (*Constitution* 1874, Art. XIV, Sec. 1.)

California: "A general diffusion of knowledge and intelligence being essential to the preservation of the rights and liberties of the people the Legislature shall encourage by all suitable means the promotion of intellectual, scientific, moral, and agricultural improvement." (*Constitution* 1879, Art. IX, Sec. 1.)

Idaho: "The stability of a republican form of government depending mainly upon the intelligence of the people, it shall be the duty of the legislature of Idaho to establish and maintain a general, uniform, and thorough system of public, free common schools." (*Constitution* 1890, Art. IX, Sec. 1.)

Indiana: "Knowledge and learning generally diffused through a community being essential to the preservation of a free government, and spreading the opportunities and advantages of education through the various parts of the country being highly conducive to this end, it shall be the duty of the general assembly to provide by law for the improvement of such lands as are, or hereafter may be, granted by the United States to this state, for the use of schools, and to apply any funds which may be raised from such lands or from any other quarter, to the accomplishment of the grand object for which they are or may be intended." (*Constitution* 1816, Art. IX, Sec. 1.) "Knowledge and learning generally diffused throughout a community being essential to the preservation of a free government, it shall be the duty of the general assembly to encourage, by all suitable means, moral, intellectual, scientific and agricultural improvement and to provide by law for a general, and uniform system of schools," etc. (*Constitution* 1851, Art. VIII, Sec. 1.)

Kansas: "A general diffusion of knowledge being essential to

46994

the preservation of the rights and liberties of the people, schools and the means of education shall be forever encouraged in this state." (*Constitution* 1857, Art. XIV, Sec. 1.) "The stability and perpetuity of free republican institutions depend upon the intelligence and virtue of the people, therefore, it is declared to be the duty of the State to establish by law, at the earliest possible period, a uniform system of free schools," etc. (*Constitution* 1858, Art. VII, Sec. 1.) "The legislature shall encourage the promotion of intellectual, moral, scientific, and agricultural improvement by establishing a uniform system of common schools," etc. (*Constitution* 1859, Art. VI, Sec. 2.)

Maine: "A general diffusion of the advantages of education being essential to the promotion of the rights and liberties of the people, to promote this important object, the legislature are authorized, and it shall be their duty to require the several towns to make suitable provision, at their own expense, for the support and maintenance of public schools, . . ." (*Constitution* 1820, Art. VIII.)

Minnesota: "The stability of a republican form of government depending mainly upon the intelligence of the people, it shall be the duty of the legislature to establish a general and uniform system of public schools." (*Constitution* 1857, Art. VIII, Sec. 1.)

Mississippi: "As the stability of a republican form of government depends mainly upon the intelligence and virtue of the people, it shall be the duty of the legislature to encourage, by all suitable means, the promotion of intellectual, scientific, moral, and agricultural improvement, by establishing a uniform system of free public schools," etc. (*Constitution* 1868, Art. VIII, Sec. 1.) Compare the above with the Constitution of 1832, Art. VII, Sec. 14, in which the religious element is emphasized. (Page 99.)

Missouri: "A general diffusion of knowledge and intelligence being essential to the preservation of the rights and liberties of the people, the general assembly shall establish and maintain free schools," etc. (*Constitution* 1865, Art. IX, Sec. 1, and *Constitution* 1875, *Art.* XI, Sec. 1.)

New Hampshire: "Knowledge and learning generally diffused through a community being essential to the preservation of a free government; and spreading the opportunities and advantages of education through the various parts of the country being highly conducive to promote this end, it shall be the duty of the legislators and the magistrates, in all future periods of this government, to cherish the interest of literature and the sciences, and all seminaries and public schools," etc. (*Constitution* 1784, Part II, Encouragement of Literature, etc.) Almost the same wording is found in the Constitution of 1792, Pt. 2, Sec. 83.

North Dakota: "A high degree of intelligence, patriotism, integrity, and morality on the part of every voter in a government by the people being necessary in order to insure the continuance of that government and the prosperity and happiness of the people, the legislative assembly shall make provision for the establishment and maintenance of a system of public schools," etc. (*Constitution* 1889, Art. VIII, Sec. 147.)

Rhode Island: "The diffusion of knowledge as well as of virtue among the people being essential to the preservation of their rights and liberties, it shall be the duty of the general assembly to promote public schools," etc. (*Constitution* 1842, Art. XII, Sec. 1.)

South Dakota: "The stability of a republican form of government depending on the morality and intelligence of the people, it shall be the duty of the legislature to establish and maintain a general and uniform system of public schools." (*Constitution* 1889, Art. VIII, Sec. 1.)

Tennessee: "Knowledge, learning and virtue being essential to the preservation of republican institutions, and the diffusion of the opportunities and advantages of education throughout the different portions of the state being highly conducive to the promotion of this end, it shall be the duty of the general assembly in all future periods of this government to cherish literature and science." *Constitution* 1834, Art. XI, Sec. 10.)

Texas: "A general diffusion of knowledge being essential to the preservation of the rights and liberties of the people, it shall be the duty of the legislature of this State to make suitable provisions for the support and maintenance of public schools." (*Constitution* 1845, Art. X, Sec. 1. Also *Constitution* 1866, Art. X, Sec. 1.) Practically the same wording is found in the Constitution of 1876, Article VII, Section 1.

CHAPTER XI

STATE CONSTITUTIONAL PROVISIONS

Forbidding Either Sectarian Religious Instruction or Religious Tests in Public Schools, or the Appropriation of Public Funds to Schools Under Ecclesiastical Control or Not Under the Absolute Control of the State.

Constitutional provisions forbidding either sectarian religious instruction or religious tests in public schools or the appropriation of public funds to schools under ecclesiastical control or not under the absolute control of the state exist in almost every state constitution in force at the present time. These represent, as a whole, the culmination of the struggle in which the American people have sought to establish and maintain the secular ideal of public education as a necessary instrument of democracy as opposed to that view which would make the aim and control of education wholly or partly ecclesiastical. Ordinary legislation is too easily reversed; it has been necessary to imbed these provisions for the security and permanence of our educational system and institutions in these fundamental instruments of government, the Constitutions, where they are safe from the dangers of mere legislative caprice, and where usually they can be altered only by a direct appeal to the people of entire states and by a substantial majority of their votes.

These constitutional provisions take on a variety of forms. Some are detailed and specific in their wording; there can be no doubt as to their intent. Others are general, vague, and must be supplemented by specific legislation and interpreted by the courts in order to determine just what they cover. A few include all three of the prohibitions mentioned in the title of this chapter. Others contain only one or two. The most common form is that prohibiting the appropriation of public funds to sectarian institutions. This is found in the constitutions of over forty states. Sometimes this prohibition may be set aside by a two-thirds vote of the state legislature. Sometimes the prohibition is limited to the income from special school funds, or to money appropriated by the state to smaller political divisions for educational purposes. Again the prohibition extends to all funds, however derived, and to all political subdivisions of the state, as well as to the state itself. The common method for enforcing the prohibitions against sectarian instruction, and the establishment of religious tests is to threaten to withhold the state appropriations from the offending school authorities.

Alabama: " No appropriation shall be made to any charitable or educational institution not under the absolute control of the state, other than normal schools established by law for the professional training of teachers for the public schools of the state, except by a vote of two-thirds of all the members elected to each house." (*Constitution* 1875, Art. IV, Sec. 34.) " No money raised for the support of the public schools of the state shall be appropriated to or used for the support of any sectarian or denominational school." (*Constitution* 1875, Art. XII, Sec. 8.) These provisions are repeated in the *Constitution* of 1901, Sec. 73 and Sec. 263.

Arizona: " No public money or property shall be appropriated for or applied to any religious worship, exercise, or instruction, or to the support of any religious establishment." (*Constitution* 1910, Art. II, Declaration of Rights, Sec. 12.) " No tax shall be laid, or appropriation of public money made in aid of any church, or private or sectarian school, or any public service corporation." (*Constitution* 1910, Art. IX, Sec. 9.) " No sectarian instruction shall be imparted in any school or State educational institution that may be established under this Constitution, and no religious or political test or qualification shall ever be required as a condition of admission into any public educational institution of the State, as teacher, student, or pupil; but the liberty of conscience hereby secured shall not be so construed as to justify practices or conduct inconsistent with the good order, peace, morality, or safety of the State, or with the rights of others." (*Constitution* 1910, Art. XI, Sec. 7.) " Provision shall be made by law for the establishment and maintenance of a system of public schools which shall be open to all the children of the State and be free from sectarian control and said schools shall always be conducted in English." (*Constitution* 1910, Art. XXII, Sec. 7.)

Arkansas: ". . . but no religious or other sect or sects shall ever have any exclusive right to, or control of, any part of the school funds of this state." (*Constitution* 1868, Art. IX, Sec. 1.) The foregoing is omitted from the constitution of 1874 where we find the following: " No money or property belonging to the public school fund, or to this state for the benefit of schools or universities shall ever be used for any other than for the respective purposes to which it belongs." (*Constitution* 1874, Art. XIV, Sec. 3.)

California: "No public money shall ever be appropriated for the support of any sectarian or denominational school or any school not under the exclusive control of the officers of the public schools; nor shall any sectarian or denominational doctrine be taught, or instruction therein be permitted, directly or indirectly, in any of the common schools of this state." (*Constitution* 1879, Art. IX, Sec. 8.)

Colorado: " No appropriation shall be made for charitable, industrial, educational, or benevolent purposes, to any person, corporation, or community not under the absolute control of the state, nor to any denominational or sectarian institution or association." (*Constitution* 1876, Art. V, Sec. 34.) " Neither the general assembly nor any county, city, town, township, school district, or other public corporation shall ever make any appropriation or pay from any public fund or moneys whatever, anything in aid of any church or sectarian society, or for any sectarian purpose, or to help support or sustain any school, academy, seminary, college, university, or other literary or scientific institution, controlled by any church, or sectarian denomination whatsoever; nor shall any grant or donation of land, money or other personal property, ever be made by the state or any such public corporation to any church or for any sectarian purpose." (*Constitution* 1876, Art. IX, Sec. 7.) " No religious test or qualification shall ever be required of any person as a condition of admission into any public educational institution of the state, either as teacher or student; and no teacher or student of any such institution shall ever be required to attend or participate in any religious service whatsoever. No sectarian tenets or doctrines shall ever be taught in the public schools, nor shall any distinction or classification of pupils be made on account of race or color." (*Constitution* 1876, Art. IX, Sec. 8.)

Connecticut: "The fund called the school fund shall remain a perpetual fund, the interest of which shall be inviolably appropriated to the support and encouragement of the public or common schools throughout the State, and for the equal benefit of all the people thereof. The value and amount of said fund shall as soon as practicable be ascertained in such manner as the general assembly may prescribe, published, and recorded in the controller's office; and no law shall ever be made, authorizing said fund to be diverted to any other use than the encouragement and support of public or common schools, among the several school societies as justice and equity shall require." (*Constitution* 1818, Art. VIII, Sec. 2.)

Delaware: "No portion of any fund now existing or which may hereafter be appropriated, or raised by tax for educational purposes, shall be appropriated to, or used by, or in aid of any sectarian, church, or denominational school; provided that all real or personal property used for school purposes, where the tuition is free, shall be exempt from taxation and assessment for public purposes." (*Constitution* 1897, Art. X, Sec. 3.) "No part of the principal or income of the public school fund, now or hereafter existing, shall be used for any other purpose than the support of free public schools." (*Constitution* 1897, Art. X, Sec. 4.)

Florida: "No preference shall ever be given by law to any church, sect, or mode of worship, and no money shall ever be taken from the public treasury directly or indirectly in aid of any church, sect, or religious denominations, or in aid of any sectarian institution." (*Constitution* 1887, Dec. Rights, Sec. 6.) "The state school fund, the interest of which shall be exclusively applied to the support and maintenance of public, free schools shall be derived from the following sources," etc. (*Constitution* 1887, Art. XII, Sec. 4.) "No law shall be enacted authorizing the diversion or the lending of any county or district school funds, or the appropriation of any part of the permanent or available school fund to any other than school purposes; nor shall the same nor any part thereof, be appropriated to or used for the support of any sectarian school." (*Constitution* 1887, Art. XII, Sec. 13.)

Georgia: " No vote, resolution, law, or order shall pass, granting a donation, or gratuity, in favor of any person, except by the concurrence of two-thirds of each branch of the general assembly, nor by any vote to a sectarian corporation or association." (*Constitution* 1868, Art. VI, Sec. VI, Two.) " No money shall ever be taken from the public treasury, directly or indirectly, in aid of any church, sect, or denomination of religionists, or of any sectarian institution." (*Constitution* 1877, Art. I, Bill of Rights, Par. 14.)

Idaho: " The public school fund of the state shall forever remain inviolate and intact; the interest thereon only shall be expended in the maintenance of the schools of the state and shall be distributed among the several counties and school districts of the state in such manner as shall be prescribed by law. No part of this fund, principal or interest, shall ever be transferred to any other fund, or used or appropriated except as herein provided. The state treasurer shall be the custodian of this fund, and the same shall be securely and profitably invested as may be by law directed. The state shall supply all losses thereof that may in any manner occur." (*Constitution* 1890, Art. IX, Sec. 3.) " Neither the legislature nor any county, city, town, township, school district, or other public corporation shall ever make any appropriation or pay from any public fund or moneys whatever, anything in aid of any church, or sectarian or religious society or for any church or sectarian purpose, or to help support or sustain any school, academy, seminary, college, university or other literary or scientific institution controlled by any church or sectarian or religious denomination whatsoever; nor shall any grant or donation of land, money or other personal property ever be made by the state or any such public corporation to any church or for any sectarian or religious purpose." (*Constitution* 1890, Art. IX, Sec. 5.) " No religious test or qualification shall ever be required of any person as a condition of admission into any public educational institution of the state, either as teacher or student; and no teacher or student of any such institution shall ever be required to attend or participate in any religious service whatever. No sectarian or religious tenets or doctrines shall ever be taught in the public schools, nor shall any distinction or classification of pupils be made on account of race or color. No books, papers, tracts, or documents of a political, sectarian or denominational character shall be used or introduced in any schools established under the provisions of this article, nor shall any teacher or any district receive any of the public school moneys in which the schools have not been taught in accordance with the provisions of this article." (*Constitution* 1890, Art. IX, Sec. 6.)

Illinois: " Neither the general assembly nor any county, city, town, township, school district or other public corporation shall ever make any appropriation or pay from any public fund whatever, anything in aid of any church or sectarian purpose, or to help support or sustain any school, academy, seminary, college, university, or other literary or scientific institution, controlled by any church or sectarian denomination whatever; nor shall any grant or donation of land, money, or other personal property ever be made by the state or any such corporation to any church or for any sectarian purpose." (*Constitution* 1870, Art. VIII, Sec. 3.)

Indiana: " The principal of the common school fund shall remain a perpetual fund, which may be increased, but shall never be diminished, and the income thereof shall be inviolably appropriated to the support of common schools and to no other purpose whatever." (*Constitution* 1851, Art. VIII, Sec. 3.) " No money shall be drawn from the treasury for the benefit of any religious or theological institution." (*Constitution* 1851, Art. I, Sec. 6.)

Iowa: " The general assembly shall encourage by all suitable means, the promotion of intellectual, scientific, moral, and agricultural improvement. The proceeds of all lands that have been, or hereafter may be granted by the United States to this State for the support of schools . . . shall be and remain a perpetual fund, the interest of which, together with all the rents of the unsold lands, and such other means as the general assembly may provide, shall be inviolably appropriated to the support of common schools throughout the State." (*Constitution* 1857, Art. IX, Par. 2, Sec. 3.)

Kansas: ". . . but no religious or other sect or sects shall ever have any exclusive right to or control of any part of the school funds of this state." (*Constitution* 1855, Art. VII, Sec. 2.) " No religious sect or sects shall ever have any right or control of any part of the school funds of this state." (*Constitution* 1858, Art. VII, Sec. 5.) " No religious sect or sects shall ever control any part of the common school or university funds of the state." (*Constitution* 1859, Art. 6, Sec. 8.)

Kentucky: " The capital of the fund called and known as the Common School Fund, . . . shall be held inviolate for the purpose of sustaining a system of common schools. The interest and dividends of said fund together with any sum that may be produced for that purpose by taxation or otherwise, may be appropriated in aid of common schools but for no other purpose." (*Constitution* 1850, Art. XI, Sec. 1.) " The bonds of the commonwealth issued in favor of the Board of Education for the sum of $1,327,000.00 shall constitute one bond of the commonwealth in favor of the board of education, and this bond and the $73,500.00 of the stock in the Bank of Kentucky held by the Board of Education, and its proceeds shall be held inviolate for the purpose of sustaining the system of common schools. The interest and dividends of said funds together with any sum which may be produced by taxation or otherwise for purposes of common school education shall be appropriated to the common schools and to no other purpose." (*Constitution* 1891, Sec. 184.) " No portion of any fund or tax now existing or that may be hereafter raised or levied for educational purposes shall be appropriated to or used by or in aid of any church, sectarian, or denominational school." (*Constitution* 1891, Sec. 189.)

Louisiana: The growth of public sentiment in favor of secular schools is well illustrated in the successive constitutions of Louisiana, beginning with that of 1845. " The legislature shall establish free public schools throughout the state, and shall provide means

for their support . . ." (*Constitution* 1845, Title VII, Sec. 134.)
" The proceeds of all lands heretofore granted by the United
States to this State for the use or support of schools . . ., and
the proceeds of the estates of deceased persons to which the State
may become entitled by law, shall be held by the State as a loan
and shall be and remain a perpetual fund on which the State shall
pay an annual interest of six per cent; which interest together
with all the rents of the unsold lands, shall be appropriated to the
support of such schools, and this appropriation shall remain in-
violable." (*Constitution* 1845, Title VII, Sec. 135.)   Practically
the same provision is found in the Constitution of 1852, Title
VIII, Art. 137, and in the Constitution of 1864, Title XI, Art.
144.   " No appropriation shall be made by the legislature for the
support of any private school or institution whatever, but the
highest encouragement shall be granted to public schools throughout the State." (*Constitution* 1864, Title XI, Art. 146.)   The
Constitution of 1868 contains practically the same provision in
Title VII, Art. 139-140.   " No funds raised for the support of
the public schools of the state shall be appropriated to or used for
the support of any private or sectarian schools." (*Constitution*
1879, Art. 228.   Also *Constitution* 1898, Art. 253.)

Maine: " No donation, grant or endowment shall at any time
be made by the legislature to any literary institution now established, or which may hereafter be established, unless at the time
of making such endowment, the legislature of the State shall have
the power to grant any further powers to grant or alter, limit or
restrain any of the powers vested in any such literary institution
as shall be judged necessary to promote the best interests
thereof." (*Constitution* 1820, Art. VIII.)

Massachusetts: "All moneys raised by taxation in the towns
and cities for the support of public schools, and all moneys
which may be appropriated by the State for the support of common schools, shall be applied to and expended in no other
schools than those which are conducted according to law, under
the order and superintendence of the authorities of the town or
city in which the money is to be expended: and such moneys
shall never be appropriated to any religious sect for the maintenance, exclusively, of its own school." (*Constitution* 1780,
Amendment to Art. XVIII, Adopted 1855.)

Michigan: " No money shall be drawn from the treasury for the benefit of religious societies, or theological or religious seminaries." (*Constitution* 1835, Art. I, Sec. 5.) " No money shall be appropriated or drawn from the treasury for the benefit of any religious sect or society, theological or religious seminary, nor shall property belonging to the state be appropriated for any such purpose." (*Constitution* 1850, Art. IV, Sec. 40, and *Constitution* 1909, Art. II, Sec. 3.)

Minnesota: " . . . nor shall any money be drawn from the treasury for the benefit of any religious societies or religious or theological seminaries." (*Constitution* 1875, Art. I, Sec. 16.) " But in no case shall the moneys derived as aforesaid or any portion thereof, or any public moneys or property, be appropriated or used for the support of schools wherein the distinctive doctrines, creed, or tenets of any particular Christian or other religious sect are promulgated or taught." (*Constitution* 1857, Art. VIII, Sec. 3. Adopted Nov. 6, 1877.)

Mississippi: " No religious sect or sects shall ever control any part of the school or university funds of this state." (*Constitution* 1868, Art. VIII, Sec. 9.) " No religious test as a qualification for office shall ever be required; and no preference shall be given by law to any religious sect or mode of worship; but the free enjoyment of all religious sentiments and the different modes of worship shall be held sacred. The rights hereby secured shall not be construed to justify acts of licentiousness injurious to morals or dangerous to the peace and safety of the state, or to exclude the Holy Bible from use in any public school of this state." (*Constitution* 1890, Art. III, Sec. 18.) " No law granting a donation or gratuity in favor of any person or object shall be enacted, except by the concurrence of two-thirds of each branch of the legislature, nor by any vote for a sectarian purpose or use." (*Constitution* 1890, Art. III, Sec. 66.) " No religious sect or sects shall ever control any part of the school or other educational funds of this state; nor shall any funds be appropriated toward the support of any sectarian school," etc. (*Constitution* 1890, Art. VIII, Sec. 208.)

Missouri: " Neither the general assembly, nor any county,

city, town, township, or school district or other municipal corporation shall ever make an appropriation or pay from any public fund whatever, anything in aid of any religious creed, church, or sectarian purpose, or help to support or sustain any private or public school, academy, seminary, college, university, or other institution of learning controlled by any religious creed, church, or sectarian denomination whatever; nor shall any grant or donation of personal property or real estate ever be made by the state or any county, city, town, or other municipal corporation, for any religious creed, church, or sectarian purpose whatever." (*Constitution* 1875, Art. XI, Sec. 11.)

Montana: "No appropriation shall be made for charitable, industrial, educational or benevolent purposes to any person, corporation, or community not under the absolute control of the state, nor to any denominational or sectarian institution or association." (*Constitution* 1889, Art. V, Sec. 35.) "Neither the legislative assembly nor any county, city, town, or school district or other public corporation shall ever make directly or indirectly any appropriation or pay from any public fund or moneys whatever, or make any grant of lands or other property, in aid of any church or for any sectarian purpose, or to aid in the support of any school, academy, seminary, college, university, or other literary or scientific institution controlled in whole or in part by any church, sect, or denomination whatever." (*Constitution* 1889, Art. XI, Sec. 8.) "No religious or partisan test or qualification shall ever be required of any person as a condition of admission into any public educational institution of the state, either as teacher or student; nor shall attendance be required at any religious service whatever, nor shall any sectarian tenets be taught in any public educational institution of the state," etc. (*Constitution* 1889, Art. XI, Sec. 9.)

Nebraska: "The legislature shall make such provision by taxation or otherwise as with the income arising from the school trust-fund will secure a thorough and efficient system of common schools throughout the State; but no religious sect or sects shall ever have any exclusive right to or control of any part of the school-funds of this State." (*Constitution* 1866, Art. II, Education, Sec. 1.) "No sectarian instruction shall be allowed in any school or institution supported in whole or in part by the public funds set apart for educational purposes; nor shall the state accept any grant, conveyance, or bequest of money, lands or other property to be used for sectarian purposes." (*Constitution* 1875, Art. VIII, Sec. 11.)

Nevada: " The legislature shall provide for a uniform system of common schools by which a school shall be established and maintained in each school district at least six months in every year; and any school district neglecting to establish and maintain such a school, or which shall allow instruction of a sectarian character therein may be deprived of its portion of the public school fund during such neglect or infraction." (*Constitution* 1864, Art. XI, Par. 150.) " No sectarian instruction shall be imparted or tolerated in any school or university that may be established under this constitution." (*Constitution* 1864, Art. XI, Par. 157.) " No public funds of any kind or character whatever, state, county, or municipal, shall be used for sectarian purposes." (*Constitution* 1864, Art. XI, Par. 158. Added in 1880.)

New Hampshire: " No money raised by taxation shall ever be granted or applied for the use of the schools or institutions of any religious sect or denomination." (*Constitution* 1792, Art. 82, Amendment of 1877.)

New Jersey: " The fund for the support of free schools, . . . shall be securely invested and remain a perpetual fund; and the income thereof, except so much as it may be judged expedient to apply to an increase of the capital, shall be annually appropriated to the support of public, free schools for the equal benefit of all the people of the state, and it shall not be competent for the legislature to borrow, appropriate or use the said fund, or any part thereof, for any other purpose, under any pretence whatever." (*Constitution* 1844, Art. IV, Sec. 6. As amended 1875.)

New Mexico: " No appropriation shall be made for charitable, educational, or other benevolent purposes to any person, corporation, association, institution, or community not under the absolute control of the state, but the legislature may, in its discretion, make appropriations for the charitable institutions and hospitals for the maintenance of which annual appropriations were made by the legislative assembly of nineteen hundred and nine." (*Constitution* 1911, Art. IV, Sec. 31.) " The schools, colleges, universities, and other educational institutions provided for by this constitution shall forever remain under the exclusive control of the State, and no part of the proceeds arising from the sale or disposal of any lands granted to the State by Congress, or any other fund appropriated, levied, or collected for educational purposes, shall be used for the support of any sectarian, denominational, or private school, college, or university." (*Constitution* 1911, Art. XII, Sec. 3.) " No religious test shall ever be required as a condition of admission into the public schools or any educational institution of this State, either as a teacher or student, and no teacher or student of such school or institution shall ever be required to attend or participate in any religious service whatsoever." (*Constitution* 1911, Art. XII, Sec. 9.)

New York: " Neither the state nor any sub-division thereof, shall use its property or credit or any public money, or authorize or permit either to be used, directly or indirectly, in aid or maintenance, other than for examination or inspection, of any school or institution of learning wholly or in part under the control or direction of any religious denomination or in which any denominational tenet or doctrine is taught." (*Constitution* 1894, Art. IX, Sec. 4.)

North Carolina: " The proceeds of all lands that have been or hereafter may be granted by the United States to this State, . . . also all money, stocks, bonds, and other property, now belonging to any State fund for purposes of education; also the net proceeds of all sales of the swamp lands belonging to the State, and all other grants, gifts or devises, that have been or hereafter may be made to this State . . .; together with so much of the ordinary revenue of the State as may be by law set apart for that purpose, shall be faithfully appropriated for establishing and maintaining in this State a system of free public schools, and for no other uses or purposes whatsoever." (*Constitution* 1876, Art. IX, Sec. 4.)

North Dakota: "A high degree of intelligence, patriotism, integrity, and morality on the part of every voter in a government of the people being necessary in order to insure the maintenance of that government and the prosperity and happiness of the people, the legislative assembly shall make provision for the establishment and maintenance of a system of public schools, which shall be open to all children of the state of North Dakota and free from sectarian control. This legislative requirement shall be irrevocable without the consent of the United States and the people of North Dakota." (*Constitution* 1889, Art. VIII, Sec. 147.) "All colleges, universities, and other educational institutions for the support of which lands have been granted to this state, or which are supported by a public tax, shall remain under the absolute and exclusive control of the state. No money raised for the support of the public schools of the state shall be appropriated to or used for the support of any sectarian school." (*Constitution* 1889, Sec. 152.)

Ohio: "But no religious or other sect or sects, shall ever have any exclusive right to or control of, any part of the school funds of this state." (*Constitution* 1851, Art. VI, Sec. 2.)

Oklahoma: "Provision shall be made for the establishment and maintenance of a system of public schools, which shall be open to all the children of the state and free from sectarian control." (*Constitution* 1907, Art. I, Sec. 5.) "No public money or property shall ever be appropriated, applied, donated, or used, directly or indirectly, for the use, benefit, or support of any sect, church, denomination, or system of religion, or for the use, benefit, or support, of any priest, preacher, minister, or other religious teacher, or sectarian institution as such." (*Constitution* 1907, Art. II, Sec. 5.) "The interest and income of the permanent school fund, the net income from the leasing of public lands which may have been or may be granted by the United States to the state for the use and benefit of the common schools, together with any revenues derived from taxes authorized to be levied for such purposes; and any other sums which may be added thereto by law, shall be used and applied each year for the benefit of the common schools of the state, and shall be for this purpose apportioned among and between all the common school districts of the state, in proportion to the school population of the several districts; and no part of the fund shall ever be diverted from this purpose, or used for any other purpose than the support and maintenance of common schools for the equal benefit of all the people of the state." (*Constitution* 1907, Art. XI, Sec. 3.)

Oregon: "No money shall be drawn from the treasury for the benefit of any religious or theological institution, nor shall any money be appropriated for the payment for any religious services in either house of the legislative assembly." (*Constitution* 1857, Bill of Rights, Art. I, Sec. 5.)

Pennsylvania: "No money raised for the support of the public schools of the commonwealth shall be appropriated to or used for the support of any sectarian school." (*Constitution* 1874, Art. X, Sec. 2.)

Rhode Island: "The money which now is or which may hereafter be appropriated by law for the establishment of a permanent fund for the support of public schools, shall be securely invested, and remain a perpetual fund for that purpose. The general assembly shall not divert said money or fund from the aforesaid uses, nor borrow, appropriate, or use the same, or any part thereof, for any other purpose under any pretense whatsoever." (*Constitution* 1843, Art. XII, Sec. 2-4)

South Carolina: "No religious sect or sects shall have exclusive right to or control of any part of the school funds of the state, nor shall sectarian principles be taught in the public schools." (*Constitution* 1868, Art. X, Sec. 5, and *Constitution* 1894, Art. X, Sec. 5.)

South Dakota: "No money or property of the state shall be given or appropriated for the benefit of any sectarian or religious society or institution." (*Constitution* 1889, Bill of Rights, Art. VI, Sec. 3.) "The income and interest of this fund, etc., shall be faithfully used and applied each year for the benefit of the public schools of the state, . . . , and no part of the fund, either principal or interest, shall ever be diverted even temporarily, from this purpose, or used for any other purpose whatever, than the maintenance of public schools for the equal benefit of all the people of the state." (*Constitution* 1889, Art. VIII, Sec. 3.) "No appropriation of lands, money, or other property or credits to aid any sectarian school shall ever be made by the state or any county or municipality within the state, nor shall the state nor any county or municipality within the state accept any grant, conveyance, gift, or bequest of lands, money, or other property to be used for sectarian purposes, and no sectarian instruction shall be allowed in any school or institution aided or supported by the state." (*Constitution* 1889, Art. VIII, Sec. 16.)

Tennessee: " The fund called the common school fund, . . . shall remain a perpetual fund, the principal of which shall never be diminished by legislative appropriation; and the interest thereof shall be inviolably appropriated to the support and encouragement of common schools throughout the state, and for the equal benefit of all the people thereof; and no law shall be made authorizing said fund or any part thereof to be diverted to any other use than the support and encouragement of common schools." (*Constitution* 1870, Art. XI, Sec. 12.)

Texas: "And it shall be the duty of the legislature to set apart not less than one tenth of the annual revenue of the state derivable from taxation, as a perpetual fund, which fund shall be appropriated to the support of free, public schools, and no law shall ever be made diverting said fund to any other use." (*Constitution* 1845, Art. X, Sec. 2.) " The principal of all bonds and other funds, and the principal arising from the sale of the lands herein before set apart to said school fund, shall be the permanent school fund; and all the interest derivable therefrom and the taxes herein authorized and levied shall be the available school fund, which shall be applied annually to the support of the public free schools. And no law shall ever be enacted appropriating any part of the permanent or available school fund to any other purpose whatever; nor shall the same nor any part thereof, ever be applied to or used for the support of any sectarian school; and the available school fund herein provided shall be distributed to the several counties according to their scholastic populations and applied in such manner as may be provided by law." (*Constitution* 1876, Art. VII, Sec. 5. Added 1891.)

Utah: " No public money or property shall be appropriated for or applied to any religious worship, exercise, or institution, or for the support of any ecclesiastical establishment." (*Constitution* 1895, Art. I, Sec. 4.) " The legislature shall provide for the establishment and maintenance of a uniform system of public schools which shall be open to all children of the state and free from sectarian control." (*Constitution* 1895, Art. X, Sec. 1.) " Neither religious nor partisan test or qualification shall be required of any person, as a condition of admission, as teacher or student, into any public educational institution of the state." (*Constitution* 1895, Art. X, Sec. 12.) " Neither the legislature nor any county, city, town, school district or other public corporation shall make any appropriation to aid in the support of any school, seminary, academy, college, university, or other institution, controlled in whole or in part by any church, sect or denomination whatever." (*Constitution* 1895, Art. X, Sec. 13.)

Virginia: " No appropriation of public funds shall be made to any school or institution of learning not owned or exclusively controlled by the state or some political division thereof; provided, 1st that the general assembly may in its discretion continue the appropriations to the College of William and Mary; . . . 3rd counties, cities, towns, or districts may make appropriations to non-sectarian schools of manual, industrial, or technical training and also to any school or institution of learning owned or exclusively controlled by such county, city, town or school district." (*Constitution* 1902, Art. 9, Sec. 141.)

Washington: " The principal of the common school fund shall remain permanent and irreducible. The legislature may make further provision for enlarging said fund. The interest accruing on said fund together with all rentals and other revenues derived therefrom, and from lands and other property devoted to the common school fund, shall be exclusively applied to the current use of the common schools." (*Constitution* 1889, Art. IX, Sec. 3.) "All schools maintained or supported wholly or in part by the public funds shall be forever free from sectarian control or influence." (*Constitution* 1889, Art. IX, Sec. 4.)

West Virginia: " The existing permanent and invested school fund . . . .; all grants, devises, or bequests that may be made to this State for the purposes of education, ...; this State's just share of the literary fund of Virginia . . . .; and such sums as may from time to time, be appropriated by the legislature for the purpose, shall be set apart as a separate fund, to be called the ' school fund,' . . . .; and the interest thereof shall be annually applied to the support of free schools throughout the State, and to no other purpose whatever." (*Constitution* 1872, Art. XII, Sec. 4.)

Wisconsin: "Nor shall any money be drawn from the treasury for the benefit of religious societies, or religious or theological seminaries." (*Constitution* 1848, Art. I, Sec. 18.) "The legislature shall provide for the establishment of district schools which shall be as nearly uniform as practicable; and such schools shall be free and without charge for tuition to all children between the ages of four and twenty years, and no sectarian instruction shall be allowed therein." (*Constitution* 1848, Art. X, Sec. 3.) "Provision shall be made by law for the establishment of a state university at or near the seat of state government, and for connecting with the same from time to time such colleges in different parts of the state as the interests of education may require. The proceeds of all lands that have been or may hereafter be granted by the United States to the state for the support of a university shall be and remain a perpetual fund called the university fund, the interest of which shall be appropriated to the support of the state university, and no sectarian instruction shall be allowed in such university." (*Constitution* 1848, Art. X, Sec. 6.)

Wyoming: "No money of the state shall ever be given or appropriated to any sectarian or religious society or institution." (*Constitution* 1889, Art. I, Sec. 19.) "No appropriation shall be made for charitable, industrial, educational, or benevolent purposes to any person, corporation or community not under the absolute control of the state, nor to any denominational or sectarian institution or association." (*Constitution* 1889, Art. III, Sec. 36.) "Nor shall any portion of the public school fund ever be used to support or assist any private school, or any school, academy, seminary, college, or other institution of learning controlled by any church, or sectarian organization or religious denomination whatsoever." (*Constitution* 1889, Art. VII, Sec. 8.) "No sectarian instruction, qualification or tests shall be imposed, exacted, applied, or in any manner tolerated in the schools of any grade or character controlled by the state, nor shall attendance be required at any religious service therein, nor shall any sectarian tenets or doctrines be taught or favored in any public school or institution that may be established under this constitution." (*Constitution* 1889, Art. VII, Sec. 12.)

CHAPTER XII

STATE SUPREME COURT DECISIONS FAVORING THE RELIGIOUS IDEAL OF EDUCATION

Since 1850 the supreme courts of no less than twenty-one states have been called upon to decide at least thirty cases involving in some form the question of the proper relation of religion and public education. Of these, seventeen cases, in fifteen states, have been decided in favor of the secular view; thirteen cases, in nine states, in favor of the religious view. In four instances there were handed down dissenting opinions, two favoring the former and two the latter view.

Chiefly, the courts have been concerned with determining: (1) What constitutes religious or sectarian religious instruction? (2) What constitutes the use of public school property for sectarian purposes? (3) What constitutes a sectarian school within the meaning of the constitutional provisions forbidding the appropriation of public funds to such? Some decisions have dealt with only one of these three phases, others have included all of them. Some have studiously confined themselves to the particular question at issue; others have faced the whole of the problem involved and have sought to lay down sound principles for dealing therewith.

In presenting the conclusions and most significant portions of these decisions, the above arrangement into three groups will be followed as far as practicable, those favoring the religious view being given first, followed by those upholding the secular view.

1. *What constitutes religious or sectarian religious instruction?*

Illinois

In McCormick *vs.* Burt decided by the supreme court of Illinois in 1880, it was held that a rule of a board of education requiring a teacher to read a chapter from the King James' version of the Bible as a part of the morning exercises was a reasonable exercise of the powers vested in the board, and neither the teacher nor the board were liable for damages for excluding from the school a pupil who refused to observe the proper decorum during such reading. (95 Illinois, p. 263.)

In the case of North *vs.* The Board of Trustees of the University of Illinois decided by the supreme court of Illinois in 1891, it was held that a rule of the trustees of the state university, requiring students to attend non-sectarian religious exercises in the university chapel, was not in conflict with the provisions of the state constitution, that " no person shall be required to attend or support any ministry or place of worship against his consent." (*Constitution* 1870, Art. 2, Par. 3.) The court further remarks that there is nothing in the constitution so far discountenancing religious worship that colleges and other public institutions of learning may not lawfully adopt all reasonable regulations for the inculcation of moral and religious principles in those attending them. (27 *Northeastern Reporter*, p. 54.)

In People *ex rel.* Ring *et al vs.* Board of Education of District 24, decided in 1910 by the supreme court of Illinois, there was a dissenting opinion concurred in by justices Hand and Cartwright from which the following are excerpts:

" The Bible is not mentioned in the Constitution, nor is there found therein any express inhibition against the giving of religious or moral instruction in the public schools, and while the Constitution is silent upon these subjects, it has been from the formation of our state government to the present time universally recognized by the people that there are certain fundamental principles of religion and morality which the safety of society requires should be imparted to the youth of the state, and that those principles may be properly taught in the public schools as a part of the secular knowledge which it is their province to instill into the youthful mind."

" It has always been understood that those general provisions found in the several state Constitutions which usually appear in what are designated as a " bill of rights," and which provide that the enjoyment of the free exercise of religious profession and worship, without discrimination, shall be forever guaranteed to the people, and that they shall not be required to attend upon or support any ministry or place of worship against their consent, were primarily designed to prevent the establishment of a state religion or the compulsion of the citizen to support, by taxation or otherwise, an established ministry or places of established worship, it being the object of such constitutional provisions to work a complete divorcement of the state and the church, and to sever the relation between the state and church which had existed in the mother country prior to the Revolution and secure to the citizen freedom of conscience in the matter of religious belief and worship, and that the instruction which was to be imparted in the public schools did not fall within those provisions of the Constitution unless the instruction sought to be imparted degenerated into what may be properly designated as denominational or sectarian instruction, and falls within the inhibitions of those provisions of the Constitution which were enacted with a view to placing all religious denominations or religious sects upon an equality before the law. . . ." " We think it obvious, therefore, that all must agree that there can be no rational constitutional basis upon which this court can hold that the Bible can be excluded from the public schools of the state other than upon the ground that it is sectarian in character and falls within those inhibitions of the state Constitution which prohibit teaching in our public schools the beliefs and doctrines of the different denominations or sects into which the believers of the Bible have in the course of time divided."

" None of the courts of last resort have held that the Bible, as an entirety, could be excluded from the public schools, upon constitutional grounds, as none of them have held that all parts of it were sectarian."

" The Supreme Court of every state of the Union which has spoken on the subject, with the exception of Wisconsin and Nebraska, has held that the reading of the Bible in the public schools is not prohibited by constitutional enactment, and the Supreme Courts of Wisconsin and Nebraska each hold that only portions of the Bible may be excluded."

" We think it is apparent that it must be held, from a constitutional standpoint, that all parts of the Bible can be read in the public schools, or that it must be excluded as an entirety from the public schools," etc.

" We do not think the Bible can be said to be a sectarian book or that its teachings are sectarian. Its plan of salvation is broad enough to include all the world, and the fact that those who believe in the Bible do not agree as to the interpretation of its teachings and have divided into sects, and are therefore sectarian in their beliefs, does not change the Bible or make it a sectarian book. To make the Bible sectarian it must be made to appear that it teaches the dogmas of some particular sect, and it is not sufficient, to show that it is sectarian, to establish that its teachings are so comprehensive that different phases of belief may be founded on argument based upon some of its parts which, when perhaps only imperfectly examined and partially understood, may seem to tend to support the doctrines of a particular sect and to overthrow the doctrines of some other sect."

" We think the great weight of authority sustains the position that the Bible, or any version thereof, may be read in the public schools of this state, without comment, without violating those inhibitions of the Constitution which prohibit the giving of sectarian religious instruction in the public schools. The opinion of the Supreme Court of Wisconsin which holds only portions of the Bible may be read in the public schools was repudiated by this court in North *vs.* Trustees of the University of Illinois, supra."

" It is urged, however, that the children of relators were required to bow their heads and assume a devotional attitude during the reading of the Bible and the recitation of the Lord's Prayer and the singing of sacred hymns. This is true in part; but the petition does not allege the relators' children were required to participate in the recitation of the Lord's Prayer or in the singing of said sacred hymns. At most, according to the averments of the petition, the children of the relators were required to remain quiet during the exercises, and the fact that they were required to bow their heads and fold their hands during the exercises did not convert the school into a place of worship."

" It is also said that some of the children in the school were asked to explain certain passages of the Bible which were read. It does not appear from the petition what the passages were which were required to be explained, what the explanation was, or that the children of relators were ever called upon by the teacher to make such explanation. We think, therefore, that the fact that some of the children in the school were required to explain the meaning of certain passages of Scripture which were read in their presence did not convert the school into a place of worship."

" Our conclusion is that the exercises which were conducted in said school did not convert the school into a place of worship which the relators' children were required to attend or the relators who were taxpayers were required to support."

" It is said in the majority opinion that a child cannot hear the Scriptures read in the public schools without being instructed as to the divinity of Jesus Christ, which would be an affront to a large and intelligent religious denomination whose members do not admit that it teaches such a doctrine, and the same may be said of the other sectarian beliefs mentioned in the opinion. Freethinkers and atheists do not constitute a sect which is an organized religious body, and the prohibition against sectarian instruction, which relates only to the teaching of the doctrine of a particular sect, has no application to them. The Constitution is not directed against the Bible, but applies equally to all forms and phases of religious beliefs. If the Bible is to be excluded because it pertains to a religion and a future state, heathen mythology must go with it. Moral philosophy must be discarded because it reasons of God and immortality, and all literature which mentions a Supreme Being, or intimates any obligations to Him, must be excluded. We cannot conceive that the framers of the Constitution, or the people, intended that the best and most inspiring literature, history, and science should be excluded from the public schools, so that nothing should be left except that which has been sterilized, so as not to interfere with the beliefs or offend the sensibilities of atheists."

" The majority opinion seems to proceed upon the theory that the people cannot be trusted to determine, through their constitutionally-elected school officers, the question whether the Bible shall be read in the public schools of the state, for fear that where Protestants are in the majority the King James' version will be read and where the Catholics are in the majority the Douay version will be read, and that by leaving the question to the determination of the school boards (where it has heretofore rested) a religious contest may be expected at each election of a school director. The principle which lies at the basis of our government is that majorities must control in the determination of all questions which affect the public, and that principle applies here as it does in the decision of all public questions. The state of Illinois is a Christian state. Its people as a people are a Bible-reading people, and its citizens who are students of and believers in the Bible are not all found in the churches. We are of the opinion the decision of the question whether the Bible shall be read in the public schools should be left where it has rested from the foundation of the state and through its entire history, i. e., with the local school boards, — and this court, with a view to foreclose the people by its decisions upon the question whether they desire to have the Bible read in the public schools, should not read into our state Constitution, as the majority opinion does, a provision excluding the Bible and all its translations from the public schools, and that especially should this be true in view of the well-known historical fact that the framers of the Constitution of 1870 expressly refused to incorporate into the Constitution a provision excluding the Bible from the public schools when that provision was offered in the convention, and declared by its action in declining to incorporate into the Constitution such provision, in view of the members of that convention, the question whether the Bible should be read in the public schools should rest with the several school boards of the state, where it had rested under the Constitutions of 1818 and 1848. While it is true this court may construe the Constitution, it has not the power, and it should not, under a pretext to construe the Constitution, amend it, and certainly not in a case like this, where the effect of the amendment will be to deprive many thousands of children living in this state of any knowledge of the principles taught in the Bible, as the Bible is not taught in all the homes of the state, and the only knowledge which a large number of children in this state will ever gain of the Bible must be through the public schools, and if they do not get such knowledge there it will be lost to them entirely. We therefore most respectfully dissent from the majority opinion, and earnestly protest against a result which excludes the Bible from the public schools of the state."[1]

[1] People *ex rel.* Ring *et al. vs.* Board of Education of District 24. *Northeastern Reporter,* Vol. 92, No. 5 August 2, 1910. West Pub. Co. St. Paul, Minn.

Iowa

In Moore *vs.* Monroe decided by the supreme court of Iowa in 1884 the facts were as follows: The plaintiff, a citizen and patron of the Bloomfield Independent School District, brought an action against the teachers of the school and the directors of the district praying for an injunction to prevent the reading of the Bible or any part thereof in the school and to prevent the singing of religious songs in school. The teachers were accustomed to occupy a few minutes each morning in reading selections from the Bible, in repeating the Lord's Prayer, and singing religious songs. The plaintiff had two children in school but they were not required to be present during these exercises. The plaintiff objected to this procedure and requested the teachers to stop it; they refused to do so, and the directors refused to act in the matter.

The court held that under section 1764 of the Code of Iowa it was a matter of individual option with the teachers whether they would use the Bible in school or not, such option being restricted only by the provision that no pupil should be required to read it contrary to the wishes of his parent or guardian.

The purpose of Art. I, Sec. 3, of the Bill of Rights was not to prevent the casual use of a public building as a place for offering prayer, or doing other acts of religious worship, but to prevent the enactment of law whereby any person could be compelled to pay taxes for building or repairing any place designed to be used distinctly as a place of worship. It was designed to secure citizens against taxation for religious purposes, and not for the purpose of suppressing religion itself; and it does not afford a ground for enjoining religious exercises in public schools where it appears that the burden of taxation is not increased and that plaintiff's children are not required to be present and take part in such exercises. The court refused to interfere. (64 Iowa, p. 367.)

Kansas

In Billard *vs.* Board of Education, decided by the supreme court of Kansas in 1904, the following were the facts: A boy who was disorderly during the opening exercises of the school, consisting of repeating the Lord's Prayer, a psalm, and music, was first warned and then expelled from the school. The school board notified him that he could not come back until he was ready to comply with the regulations of the school. He was required only to be orderly and to refrain from studying during the opening exercises.

The court declared that there was nothing in the state constitution excluding the Bible from the public schools, and that a teacher who for the purpose of quieting the pupils, and preparing them for their regular studies, repeated the Lord's Prayer and the Twenty-Third Psalm as a morning exercise, without comment or remark, in which none of the pupils were required to participate, was not conducting a form of religious worship or teaching sectarian or religious doctrine. (*76 Pacific Reporter,* p. 422.)

Kentucky

In Hackett *vs.* Brookville Graded School District, decided in 1905, the State Court of Appeals of Kentucky held that a public school opened with prayer and the reading, without comment, of passages from the King James' translation of the Bible, during which pupils are not required to attend, is not a place of worship, nor are its teachers ministers of religion within the meaning of the constitutional provision that no person shall be compelled to attend any place of worship or contribute to the support of a minister of religion.

A prayer offered at the opening of a public school, imploring the aid and presence of the Heavenly Father during the day's work, asking for wisdom, patience, mutual love and respect, looking forward to a heavenly reunion after death, and concluding in Christ's name, was not sectarian and did not constitute the school a sectarian school within the meaning of the constitutional provision prohibiting the appropriation of funds in aid of sectarian schools.

" The King James' translation of the Bible, or any edition of the Bible, is not a sectarian book, and the reading thereof, without comment, does not constitute sectarian instruction within the meaning of the Kentucky Statutes of 1903, Par. 4368, providing that no books of a sectarian character shall be used in any common school nor shall any sectarian doctrine be taught therein."

" We believe the reason and weight of the authorities support the view that the Bible is not of itself a sectarian book, and, when used merely for reading in the common schools, without note or comment by teachers, is not sectarian instruction; nor does such use of the Bible make the school house a house of religious worship." (87 *Southwestern Reporter,* p. 792.)

Maine

One of the earliest decisions is that of the supreme court of Maine in the case of Donahue *vs.* Richards, decided in 1854. The superintending school committee of the town of Ellsworth, Maine, directed that the English Protestant version of the Bible should be used in all the public schools of the town and that all who were of sufficient capacity to read therein would be required to read that version in school.

A child of Catholic parentage refused to read from the version of the Bible prescribed, but offered to read from the Douay version, alleging conscientious scruples. The child was expelled from school by the school committee for such refusal. It was argued that a religious test was thus set up in order to enable one to enjoy the benefits of the public schools.

The court held that the power to select books and require them to be read was vested by law in the school committee and that the court could not interfere therewith. That uniformity of reading books was a reasonable and necessary requirement. That the use of the Bible as a reading book was not interference with religious belief any more than was the reading of Roman or Grecian mythology.

" The common schools are not for the purpose of instruction in the theological doctrines of any religion or of any sect. The state regards no one sect as superior to any other and no theological view as peculiarly entitled to precedence. It is no part of the duty of the instructor to give theological instruction — and if the peculiar tenets of any particular sect were so taught it would furnish a well-grounded cause of complaint on the part of those who entertained different or opposing religious sentiments."

" But the instruction here given is not in fact, and is not alleged to have been, in articles of faith. No theological doctrines were taught. The creed of no sect was affirmed or denied.

The truth or falsehood of the book in which the school were required to read was not asserted."

"As the existence of conscientious scruples as to the reading of a book can only be known from the assertion of the child, its mere assertion must suffice for the exclusion of any book in the reading or in the hearing of which it may allege a wrong to be done to its religious conscience. The claim, so far as it may rest on conscience, is a claim to annul any regulation of the state, made by its constituted authorities. As a right existing on the part of one child, it is equally a right belonging to all. As it relates to one book, so it may apply to another — whether relating to science or morals."

" The right as claimed undermines the power of the state. It is that the will of the majority shall bow to the conscience of the minority, or of one." (38 Maine, p. 379.)

Massachusetts

In Spiller *vs.* Inhabitants of Woburn, decided by the supreme court of Massachusetts in 1866, it was held that the school committee of a town might lawfully pass an order that the schools thereof should be opened each morning with reading from the Bible and prayer, and that during the prayer each child should bow his head, unless his parents requested that he should be excused from doing so; and might lawfully exclude from the school a scholar who refused to comply with such order, and whose parents refused to request that he should be excused from doing so.

" No more appropriate method could be adopted of keeping in mind of both teachers and scholars that one of the chief objects of education, as declared by the statutes of this commonwealth and which teachers are especially enjoined to carry into effect, is to impress on the minds of children and youth committed to their care and instruction, the principles of piety, and justice, and a sacred regard for truth."

" In the first place it did not prescribe an act which was necessarily one of devotion or religious ceremony. It went no further than to require the observance of quiet and decorum during the religious service with which the school was opened. It did not compel a pupil to join in the prayer but only to assume an attitude which was calculated to prevent interruption by avoiding all communication with others during the service. In the next place the regulation did not require a pupil to comply with that part of it prescribing the position of the head during prayer, if the parent requested a child to be excused from it." (12 Allen, p. 127.)

Michigan

In the case of Pfeiffer *vs.* Board of Education of Detroit a majority of the justices of the supreme court of Michigan held in 1898 that the use in the public schools for fifteen minutes at the close of each day's session as a supplemental text book or reading of a book entitled, " Readings from the Bible," which was largely made up of extracts from the Bible emphasizing the moral precepts of the ten commandments, where the teacher was forbidden to make any comment upon the matter therein contained, and was required to excuse from that part of the session any pupil upon application of his parent or guardian, was not a violation of the state constitution, Article IV, Section 41, prohibiting the legislature from diminishing or enlarging " the civil or political rights, privileges and capacities of any person on account of his opinion or belief concerning matters of religion."

Nor was it a violation of the constitutional provision that " no money shall be appropriated or drawn from the treasury for the benefit of any religious sect or society, theological or religious seminary, nor shall property belonging to the state be appropriated to any such purpose."

Neither was it a violation of Article IV, Section 39, providing that the legislature should pass no " law to prevent any person from worshipping Almighty God according to the dictates of his own conscience, or to compel any person to attend, erect or support any place of religious worship or to pay tithes, taxes, or other rates for the support of any minister of the gospel or teacher of religion."

" The precise question is . . . whether such reading of extracts from the Bible, at which reading pupils whose faith or scruples are shocked by hearing the passage read are not required to attend, constitutes the teacher a teacher of religion, or amounts to a restriction of the civil or political rights or privileges of such students as do not attend upon the exercises."

The provision in the constitution of 1835 "meant simply that the inhabitants of the state should not be required to attend upon those church services which the people of Virginia had been by this same enactment relieved from, and that no one should be compelled to pay tithes or other rates for the support of ministers." It did not refer to schools at the time of adoption at all,— hence it does not now, is the reasoning of the court.

"In my opinion the reading of the extracts from the Bible in the manner indicated by the return, without comment, is not in violation of any constitutional provision." (118 Michigan, p. 560.)

Pennsylvania

In Hysong *vs.* Gallitzin Borough School District, decided in 1894 by the supreme court of Pennsylvania, the facts were substantially as follows: The Sisters of St. Joseph had for some years taught in the public schools at Gallitzin. For some years previous to 1894 the public school board had rented a building of the Catholic church authorities and four sisters had been employed to teach it. Protestant patrons objected to their children being put into rooms taught by the sisters. They were told there was no alternative. These teachers held certificates in their religious names granted by the county superintendent of schools after private examination at the mother house. They contracted with the directors in their religious names and used them in the transaction of any business connected with their occupation as teachers. They wore the distinctive garb and insignia of their sisterhood at all times. There was not sufficient evidence that they used it to impart sectarian, religious instruction. The Catholic catechism was taught daily in the public school room after school hours to children of Catholic parents. This was allowed by the directors. The children often studied their catechism during school hours, though the teachers forbade it. There was no religious instruction during the regular school hours. The teachers did not attend the regular institute. The school was closed on Catholic holidays. The pupils usually addressed the teachers as "Sister" and when priests visited the school they addressed them as "Father." Such teachers were employed as were detailed by the mother superior of the order to reside at Gallitzin. It was clearly the intention of the board of education to employ none other than Catholic sisters for this particular school.

A majority of the court held that the school directors might employ as teachers, sisters of a religious order of the Roman Catholic church and permit them while teaching to wear the garb of their order, providing no religious sectarian instruction was given or religious, sectarian exercises engaged in. The distinctive garb did not constitute sectarian instruction.

"Are the courts to decide that the cut of a nun's coat or the color of a woman's gown is sectarian teaching because they indicate sectarian belief? If so, then they can be called upon to go further. The religion of the teacher being known, a pure unselfish life, exhibiting itself in tenderness to the young and helpfulness for the suffering, necessarily tends to promote the religion of the man or woman who lives it. Insensibly in both young and old there is a disposition to reverence such a one, and at least to some extent, consider the life as the fruit of the particular religion. Therefore, irreproachable conduct, to that degree, is sectarian teaching. But shall the education of the children of the commonwealth be intrusted only to those men and women who are destitute of any religious belief?" (164 Pennsylvania, p. 629.)

Texas

In Church *vs.* Bullock the supreme court of Texas decided in 1908 that the " holding of morning exercises in the public schools, consisting of the reading by the teacher without comment of non-sectarian extracts from the Bible, King James' version, and repeating the Lord's prayer and singing of appropriate songs, in which the pupils are invited but not required to join does not convert the school into a sectarian or religious society, theological or religious seminary, or a sectarian school," within the meaning of the articles of the constitution, (Art. I, par. 7 and Art. 7, par. 5) "providing that no money shall be appropriated from the treasury for the benefit of any sectarian or religious society, theological or religious seminary, or for the support of any sectarian school."

" Though the citizens are entitled to the protection guaranteed by the constitution, Art. I, par. 6-7, and Art. VII, par. 5, providing that no one shall be compelled to support any place of worship, and that no money shall be appropriated from the treasury for the benefit of any religious society, yet one or more individ-

uals do not have the right to have the courts deny the people
the privilege of having their children instructed in the public
schools in the moral truths of the Bible because such objectors
do not desire that their own children shall be participants
therein."

In this case the children were not compelled to join in the
repetition of the Lord's Prayer but were requested to do so.
They were required to be present and were marked tardy if
absent from the opening exercises. The objectors were non-
believers in the Bible, Roman Catholics and Jews.

The court proceeds: " In fact Christianity is so interwoven
with the web and woof of the state government that to sustain
the contention that the constitution prohibits reading the Bible,
offering prayers, or the singing of songs of a religious character in any public school building of the government would
produce a condition bordering upon moral anarchy." (109
Southwestern Reporter, p. 115.)

2. *The use of Public School Property for Sectarian Religious
Purposes.*

Connecticut

In Scofield *vs.* the Eighth School District decided by a majority of the supreme court of Connecticut in 1858 there was a
dissenting opinion written by Justice Ellsworth and concurred
in by Justice Sanford. The following is an extract from this
opinion :

" It appears that the present and former school houses of the
district for more than half a century, have, as is usual in the
country, been used occasionally by the members of the district
for Christian worship and of late years for Sabbath schools.
This practice they wish to continue.

" Why now, I ask, may not these people be left to enjoy this
incidental advantage of what is their own, subject of course
to the vote of the district? Why not let them promote the happiness of their families and the religious training of their children as they judge wise and best?

" There is a manifest difference between a district laying a
tax to build a church edifice and occasionally using a school
house for an evening meeting, for religious edification, or instruc-

tion in sacred music. The latter is merely incidental to the main use of the building, but the former is a positive act, without law and against law." (27 Connecticut, p. 499.)

Illinois

In Nichols *vs.* School Directors the supreme court of Illinois in 1879 decided that the statutes whereby the supervision and control of school houses were vested in district school directors who might grant the temporary use of school houses when not occupied by schools, for religious meetings and Sunday schools, for evening schools and literary societies and for such other meetings as they might deem proper, was not in violation of the state constitution.

" Religion and religious worship are not so placed under the ban by the constitution that they are not allowed to become the recipients of any incidental benefit whatsoever from the public bodies or authorities of the state." (93 Illinois, p. 61.)

Iowa

In Townsend *vs.* Hagen the supreme court of Iowa decided in 1872 that the electors of a school district might legally permit the school houses in the district to be used for the purposes of religious worship and Sunday schools. The statute confers authority on the directors when legally assembled to direct the sale or other disposition of school houses that may belong to the district. (35 Iowa, p. 194.)

A similar decision was reached by the supreme court of Iowa in 1878 in the case of Davis *vs.* Boget. (50 Iowa, p. 11.)

CHAPTER XIII

STATE SUPREME COURT DECISIONS FAVORING THE SECULAR IDEAL OF EDUCATION

1. *What constitutes religious or sectarian religious instruction?*

Illinois

In the case of the People *ex rel*. Ring *et al*. *vs*. Board of Education of District 24, decided by the supreme court of Illinois, June 29, 1910, objection was raised by tax-payers, residents of the district, whose children attended the public school, to the practice of the teachers of reading before the school selected portions of the King James' version of the Bible, and requiring the pupils to recite the Lord's prayer as found in the King James' version and to sing sacred hymns, on the grounds that they and their children were members of the Roman Catholic Church, believers in its doctrines, faith and forms of worship, and that their church believed that the version of the Bible so used was an incorrect and incomplete translation; that the Lord's Prayer as used was different in wording from that taught by the Roman Catholic Church; that the laws of Illinois compelled them to send their children to school, and since there was no private or parochial school in the county, they were thus compelled to attend a place of worship against their consent, all of which was in violation of the constitutional provision securing to all the right of the free exercise and enjoyment of religious profession and worship. In a lengthy decision sustaining these objections a majority of the court uses in part the following language:

" Our Constitution guarantees the free exercise and enjoyment of religious profession and worship without discrimination. The exercises mentioned in the petition constitute worship. They are the ordinary forms of worship usually practiced by Protestant Christian denominations. Their compulsory performance would be a violation of the constitutional guaranty of the free exercise and enjoyment of religious profession and worship. One does not enjoy the free exercise of religious worship who is compelled to join in any form of religious worship."

"The wrong arises, not out of the particular version of the Bible or form of prayer used — whether that found in the Douay or the King James' version — or the particular songs sung, but out of the compulsion to join in any form of worship. The free enjoyment of religious worship includes freedom not to worship."

"It is further contended that the reading of the Bible in the schools constitutes sectarian instruction, and that thereby the provision of the Constitution is also violated which prohibits the payment from any public fund of anything in aid of any sectarian purpose. The public schools are supported by taxation, and if sectarian instruction should be permitted in them, the money used in their support would be used in aid of a sectarian purpose. The prohibition of such use of public funds is therefore a prohibition of the giving of sectarian instruction in the public schools."

"Christianity is a religion. The Catholic church and the various Protestant churches are sects of that religion. These two versions of the Scriptures are the bases of the religion of the respective sects. Protestants will not accept the Douay Bible as representing the inspired word of God. As to them it is a sectarian book containing errors and matter which is not entitled to their respect as a part of the Scriptures. It is consistent with the Catholic faith but not the Protestant. Conversely, Catholics will not accept King James' version. As to them it is a sectarian book inconsistent in many particulars with their faith, teaching what they do not believe. The differences may seem to many so slight as to be immaterial, yet Protestants are not found to be more willing to have the Douay Bible read as a regular exercise in the schools to which they are required to send their children, than are Catholics to have the King James' version read in schools which their children must attend."

"The reading of the Bible in school is instruction. Religious instruction is the object of such reading, but whether it is so or not, religious instruction is accomplished by it. The Bible has its place in the school, if it is read there at all, as the living word of God, entitled to honor and reverence. Its words are entitled to be received as authoritative and final. The reading or hearing of such words cannot fail to impress deeply the pupils' minds. It is intended and ought to so impress them. They cannot hear the Scriptures read without being instructed as to the divinity of Jesus Christ, the Trinity, the resurrection, baptism, predestination, a future state of punishments and rewards, the authority of the priesthood, the obligation and effect of the sacraments, and many other doctrines about which the various sects do not agree. Granting that instruction on these subjects is desirable, yet the sects do not agree on what instruction shall be given. Any instruction on any one of the subjects is necessarily sectarian, because, while it may be consistent with the doctrines of one or many of the sects, it will be inconsistent with the doctrines of one or more of them. The petitioners are Catholics. They are compelled by law to contribute to the maintenance of this school, and are compelled to send their children to it, or, besides contributing to its maintenance, to pay the additional expense of sending their children to another school. What right have the teachers of the school to teach those children religious doctrine different from that which they are taught by their parents? Why should the state compel them to unlearn the Lord's Prayer as taught in their homes and by their church and use the Lord's Prayer as taught by another sect? If Catholic children may be compelled to read the King James' version of the Bible in schools taught by Protestant teachers, the same law will authorize Catholic teachers to compel Protestant children to read the Catholic version. The same law which subjects Catholic children to Protestant domination in school districts which are controlled by Protestant influences will subject the children of Protestants to Catholic control where the Catholics predominate. In one part of the state the King James' version of the Bible may be read in the public schools, in another the Douay Bible, while in school districts where the sects are somewhat evenly divided, a religious contest may be expected at each election of a school director to determine which sect shall prevail in the school. Our Constitution has wisely provided against any such contest by excluding sectarian instruction altogether from the school."

" We have been considering the case of the Protestant and the Catholic. Let us consider that of the Christian and the Jew. The Christian believes that Judaism was a temporary dispensation, and that Christ was the Messiah — the Savior of the world. The Jew denies that Christ was the Messiah and regards him as an imposter. It is not the teaching of sectarian doctrine to his children to read to them daily from the New Testament, every chapter of which holds up Christ crucified as the Savior of men? "

" The only means of preventing sectarian instruction in the school is to exclude altogether religious instruction, by means of the reading of the Bible or otherwise. The Bible is not read in the public schools as mere literature or mere history. It cannot be separated from its character as an inspired book of religion. It is not adapted for use as a text book for the teaching alone of reading, of history, or of literature, without regard to its religious character. Such use would be inconsistent with its true character and the reverence in which the Scriptures are held and should be held. If any parts are to be selected for use as being free from sectarian differences of opinion, who will select them? Is it to be left to the teacher? The teacher may be religious or irreligious, Protestant, Catholic, or Jew. To leave the selection to the teacher, with no test whereby to determine the selection, is to allow any part selected to be read, and is substantially equivalent to permitting all to be read."

" It is true that this is a Christian State. The great majority of its people adhere to the Christian religion. No doubt this is a Protestant state. The majority of its people adhere to one or another of the Protestant denominations. But the law knows no distinction between the Christian and the Pagan, the Protestant and the Catholic. All are citizens. Their civil rights are precisely equal. The law cannot see religious differences, because the Constitution has definitely and completely excluded religion from the law's contemplation in considering men's rights. There can be no distinction based on religion. The state is not, and under our Constitution cannot be, a teacher of religion. All sects, religious or even anti-religious, stand on an equal footing. They have the same rights of citizenship, without discrimination. The public school is supported by the taxes which each citizen, regardless of his religion or his lack of it, is compelled to pay. The school, like the government, is simply a civil institution. It is secular, and not religious, in its purposes. The truths of the Bible are the truths of religion which do not come within the province of the public schools. No one denies their importance. No one denies that they should be taught to the youth of the state. The Constitution and the law do not interfere with such teaching, but they do banish theological polemics from the schools and the school districts. This is done, not from any hostility to religion, but because it is no part of the duty of the state to teach religion — to take the money of all, and apply it to teaching the children of all the religion of a part only. Instruction in religion must be voluntary. Abundant means are at hand for all who seek such instruction for themselves or their children. Organizations whose purpose is the spreading of religious knowledge and instruction exist, and many individuals, in connection with such organizations and independently, are devoted to that work. Religion is taught and should be taught, in the churches, Sunday schools, parochial and other church schools and religious meetings. Parents should teach it to their children at home, where its truths can be most effectively enforced. Religion does not need an alliance with the state to encourage its growth. The law does not attempt to enforce Christianity. Christianity had its beginning and grew under oppression. Where it has depended upon the sword of civil authority for its enforcement it has been weakest. Its weapons are moral and spiritual and its power is not dependent upon the force of a majority. It asks from the civil government only impartial protection and concedes to every other sect and religion the same impartial civil right."

" The Kentucky and Kansas decisions seem to consider the fact that the children of the complainants were not compelled to join in the exercises as affecting the question in some way. That suggestion seems to us to concede the position of the plaintiffs in error. The exclusion of a pupil from this part of the school exercises in which the rest of the school joins, separates him from his fellows, puts him in a class by himself, deprives him of his equality with the other pupils, subjects him to a religious stigma and places him at a disadvantage in the school, which the law never contemplated. All this is because of his religious belief. If the instruction or exercises is such that certain of the pupils must be excused from it because it is hostile to their or their parents' religious belief, then such instruction or exercise is sectarian and forbidden by the Constitution."

"In our judgment the exercises mentioned in the petition constitute religious worship, and the reading of the Bible in the school constitutes sectarian instruction."[1]

Michigan

In the case of Pfeiffer *vs.* the School Board of Detroit decided by the supreme court of Michigan in 1898 there was filed a dissenting opinion written by Justice Moore from which the following are extracts:

"We all agree that children should be carefully educated in religion. They should be taught to fear God and to love their fellow men. They should be made familiar with the truths of the Bible. They should be instructed to remember their Creator in the days of their youth, and to observe His commandments. But this is a branch of education which is not within the province of the state. It belongs to the parents, the home, the Sunday school, the mission and the church."

"The elements of our population are so diverse, comprising as it does Protestants, Roman Catholics, Hebrews, atheists, orthodox Christians, heterodox Christians, and all shades of religious belief, that no system of religion can be taught which would not be objectionable to many of them."

"It is said that the school board has removed all objection to the religious exercises embraced in the stated reading of this religious book by excusing those children whose parents may request it, from joining in it. If it is the duty of the schools under the ordinance of 1787 to teach religion it is not easy to see how this duty can be abdicated: how some can be excused from it."

He quotes from the evidence the report of the committee on school text-books made to the school board of Detroit in recommending for adoption this book, "Readings from the Bible."

[1] *Northeastern Reporter*, West Publishing Co., St. Paul, Minn, Vol. 92, No. 5. Aug. 2, 1910, p. 251-266.

" ' Your committee . . . desires to invite the consideration of the board to the matter of securing in our schools an increased attention to the principles of ethics or morals . . . an attention which should inculcate those principles of morality, and even religion, in which the great masses of our people believe and which should prevail.' "

" To so frame religious instruction or a religious exercise in the public schools as to exclude or tend to exclude any portion of the community from their enjoyment would to that extent make the teaching of the schools sectarian."

" If the state is bound to provide religious instruction, it has the right and it is its duty to decide in what religious education consists, and to say what shall be accepted as religious truth and what rejected as religious error. This, in so far as relates to schools, can only be decided by the officers under whose control the law places the schools. The result will be, where the Protestants are in the majority religious teachings acceptable to Protestants will be taught; and so, where Roman Catholics, or the Hebrews, or the people of any other religious belief, or of no belief at all, are in the majority, the minority will find taught to their children doctrines which they regard as error. A statement of the situation would seem to lead to the inevitable conclusions that religious instruction is no part of the duty of the state."

" It is said that to grant the prayer of the petitioner is, in effect, to say that the schools shall not have the benefit of the lofty truths contained in the Bible and will be deprived of its many literary and historical excellences. I cannot agree with the contention. There is a plain and practical distinction between using these selections from the Bible as the basis of a stated religious exercise, and using extracts from it incorporated into the text-books of the schools because of the moral teaching and literary excellence contained therein."

" Never at any time in the history of the world was there so much pure religion as to-day. In no country in the world are religious truths more generally entertained than in our own. In no country in the world is there so complete a separation of church and state as with us. The growth of religious truth is encouraged by religious freedom. These things were recognized and acted upon by the framers of our organic law. The religious beliefs of all persons were not simply tolerated, but were placed upon an equality by them." (118 Michigan, p. 560.)

Nebraska

In the State *ex rel*. Freeman *vs*. Scheve the supreme court of Nebraska decided as follows in 1903: " The right of the relator has been infringed. Without his consent and over his protest his children have been compelled to attend Divine worship and to participate in it.

" The regular morning exercises of the school consisted of a formal or improvised prayer, followed by the singing of Gospel Hymns. In these exercises the pupils were compelled to join, and it was their custom when prayer was offered, to rise from their seats, and stand in an attitude of reverence.

" The school being in session the right to command was vested in the teacher and the duty of obedience imposed upon the pupils. Under these conditions a request and a command were identical. A request from one in authority is understood to be a mere euphemism. It is in fact a command in inoffensive form. These children were forced to take part in religious services.

" The Bible was not read as mere literature. The reading, the prayers, and the hymns were intended to be devotional. The teacher felt it was not right to open school in any other way. It was a matter of conscience with her. It was an act of worship."

The court holds it was sectarian instruction. Exercises by a teacher in a public school, in a school building, in school hours, and in the presence of the pupils, consisting in the reading of passages from the Bible, singing of songs and hymns, offering prayer to the Deity, in accordance with the doctrines, beliefs, customs, or usages of sectarian churches or religious organizations are forbidden by the constitution of this state.

The law does not forbid the use of the Bible in either version in the schools. Because its use may be abused is no reason for shutting it out. The alleged violation must in every case be proved.

The point where the courts may rightfully interfere to prevent the use of the Bible in a public school is where legitimate use has degenerated into abuse,— " where a teacher employed to give secular instruction has violated the constitution by becoming a sectarian propagandist." (93 *Northwestern Reporter*, p. 169.)

New York

In O'Connor *vs.* Hendrick decided by the New York court of appeals in 1906 the facts were as follows: The plaintiffs duly licensed to teach entered into contracts with the board of school trustees of school district No. 9 in the town of Lima, County of Livingstone, to teach in the public school of the district for thirty-six weeks. While so engaged in teaching they wore the distinctive dress or costume of a religious society connected with the Roman Catholic church of which they were members, which society is known as the " Order of the Sisterhood of St. Joseph."

On May 28, 1903, the state superintendent of public instruction promulgated a decision made by him upon an appeal under the Consolidated School Law of 1894, p. 1278, ch. 556, Title 14, in which he declared that the wearing of an unusual dress or garb, worn exclusively by members of one religious denomination for the purpose of indicating membership in that denomination, by the teachers in the public schools, during school hours, while teaching therein, constitutes sectarian influence and the teaching of a denominational tenet or doctrine which ought not to be persisted in. The decision further declared it to be the duty of the school authorities to require such teachers to discontinue the wearing of such dress or garb while in the public schoolroom and in the performance of their duties as teachers therein, and notified one of the trustees to notify the teachers forthwith to discontinue the wearing during the school hours of each school day the distinctive dress of the sisterhood to which they belonged, and commanded him to dismiss them if they refused.

The court decided that " a regulation of the superintendent of public instruction prohibiting teachers in public schools from wearing a distinctively religious garb while teaching therein is a reasonable and valid exercise of the powers conferred upon him to establish regulations as to the management of public schools because the influence of such apparel is distinctively sectarian, and the prohibition is in accord with the public policy of the state as declared in the constitution, Art. IX, par. 4, forbidding the use of the property or credit of the state in aid of sectarian influence." (*77 Northeastern Reporter,* p. 612.)

Ohio

In the Board of Education of the City of Cincinnati *vs.* Minor decided by the supreme court of Ohio in 1872 the question involved was as to the legality of an action of the board in abolishing the reading of the Bible as a portion of the opening exercises in the schools of the city.

"The plaintiffs allege that a large majority of the children in said city, who receive any education are educated in said schools, and of said children large numbers receive no religious instruction or knowledge of the Holy Bible except that communicated as aforesaid in said schools, and that the enforcement of the resolutions first aforesaid will result in leaving such children without any religious instruction whatever. And plaintiffs allege that such instruction is necessary and indispensable to fit said children to be good citizens of the state of Ohio and of the United States, and is required by the third article of the Act passed by the Congress of the United States, July 13, 1787 entitled, 'an ordinance for the government of the territory of the United States, northwest of the River Ohio' to be forever encouraged."

With regard to the meaning of the expression, "Religion, morality and knowledge," etc., found in the constitution the court holds as follows: "The meaning is that true religion, true morality, and true knowledge shall be promoted by encouraging schools and means of instruction." "No direction is given as to what system of general knowledge or of religion or of morals shall be taught. These matters are left to legislative discretion subject to the limitations of the legislative power."

The court holds that religion does not necessarily mean the Christian religion.

"There is a total absence therefore of any legislation looking to the enforcement of religious instruction or the reading of religious books in the public schools and we are brought back to the question —What is the true meaning and effect of these constitutional provisions on this subject? Do they enjoin religious instruction in schools? and does the injunction bind the courts in the absence of legislation? We are unanimous in the opinion that both these questions must be answered in the negative." (23 Ohio, p. 211.)

Pennsylvania

In 'Hysong *vs.* Gallitzin School District determined by the supreme court of Pennsylvania in 1894, there was a dissenting opinion written by Justice Williams, with regard to the sectarian influence of the robes of the Catholic order worn by the teachers. We quote from this opinion : " No priest or bishop in full canonical dress more plainly declares his church and his office therein, than do these non-secular and ecclesiastic persons when they come into the schoolroom of a public school wearing the peculiar uniform and insignia of their sisterhood."

" If a school so conducted is not dominated by sectarian influences, and under sectarian control, it is not easy to see how it could be." (164 Pennsylvania, p. 652.)

Wisconsin

In the case of the State *ex rel.* Weiss and Others *vs.* The District School Board of Edgerton the supreme court of Wisconsin rendered in 1890 a unanimous decision concerning the constitutionality of the use of the Bible in the public schools. We quote from the decision: " The use of any version of the Bible as a text-book in the public schools and the stated reading thereof in such schools by the teachers, without restriction, though unaccompanied by any comment, has a tendency to inculcate sectarian ideas within the meaning of Sec. 3, Ch. 251, Laws of 1883, and is sectarian instruction within the meaning of Sec. 3, Art. X of the constitution."

"In considering whether such reading of the Bible is sectarian instruction the book will be regarded as a whole, because the whole Bible without exception has been designated as a text-book for the use in the Edgerton schools, and the claim of the school board is substantially, that the whole contents thereof may be so read therein if the teachers so elect. This being so it is quite immaterial if the portions thereof set out in the return as the only portions thus far read are not sectarian."

" The term sectarian instruction in the constitution manifestly refers exclusively to instruction in religious doctrines, and the prohibition is only aimed at such instruction as is sectarian: that is to say, instruction in religious doctrines which are believed by some religious sects and rejected by others. Hence to teach the existence of a supreme being of infinite wisdom, power, and goodness, and that it is the highest duty of all men to adore, obey, and love him, is not sectarian, because all religious sects so believe and teach. The instruction becomes sectarian when it goes further and inculcates doctrines or dogma concerning which the religious sects are in conflict. This we understand to be the meaning of the constitutional prohibition."

" Children of poor parents who are practically obliged to attend the public schools would if such reading were permitted, be compelled to attend a place of worship, contrary to Sec. 18, Article I of the constitution."

" The fact that children of the petitioners are at liberty to withdraw from the schoolroom during the reading of the Bible does not remove the ground of complaint."

" Furthermore there is much in the Bible which cannot be characterized as sectarian. There can be no valid objection to the use of such matter in the secular instruction of pupils. Much of it has great historical and literary value which may be thus utilized without violating the constitutional prohibition. It may also be used to inculcate good morals,— that is, our duties to each other — which may and ought to be inculcated by the district schools. No more complete code of morals exists than is contained in the New Testament, which reaffirms and emphasizes the moral obligations laid down in the ten commandments. Concerning the fundamental principles of moral ethics the religious sects do not disagree."

" Text-books founded upon the fundamental teachings of the Bible or which contain extracts therefrom, and such portions of the Bible as are not sectarian, may be used in the secular instruction of the pupils and to inculcate good morals."

A supplementary opinion was written by Justice Orton from which the following are extracts: " This case is important and timely. It brings before the courts a case of the plausible, insidious, and apparently innocent entrance of religion into our civil affairs and of an assault upon the most valuable provisions of the constitution. Those provisions should be pondered and heeded by all our people, of all nationalities and of all denominations of religion, who desire the perpetuity and value the blessings of our free government. That such is their meaning and interpretation no one can doubt, and it requires no citation of authorities to show. It is religion and sectarian instruction that are excluded by them. Morality and good conduct may be inculcated in the common schools and should be. The connection of church and state corrupts religion and makes the state despotic."

" It is said if reading the Protestant version of the Bible in school is offensive to the parents of some of the scholars, and antagonistic to their own religious views, their children can retire. They ought not to be compelled to go out of the school for such a reason for one moment. The suggestion itself concedes the whole argument. That version of the Bible is hostile to the belief of many who are taxed to support the common schools and who have equal rights and privileges in them. It is a source of religious and sectarian strife. That is enough. It violates the letter and spirit of the constitution." (76 Wisconsin, p. 177.)

2. *The use of public school property for sectarian religious purposes.*

Connecticut

In Scofield *vs.* The Eighth School District the supreme court of Connecticut held that the inhabitants of a school district had no right to use the school house of the district for religious meetings and Sunday schools against the objection of any tax payer of the district even though the district may have voted to allow such use. In this decision three out of five justices concurred. (27 Connecticut, p. 499.)

Kansas

In Spencer *vs.* The Joint School District No. 6, the supreme court of Kansas decided in 1875 that the use of a public school house for any private purpose, such as the holding of religious or political meetings, social gatherings and the like was unauthorized by law and might be restrained at the instance of any party injured thereby, and this though a majority of the electors and tax payers of the district assent to such use and an adequate rent is paid therefor. The use of a public school house for a single religious or political gathering is, legally, as unauthorized as its constant use therefor. (15 Kansas, p. 202.)

Missouri

In Dorton *vs.* Hearn decided by the supreme court of Missouri in 1878 it was held that "the board of directors of a school district cannot authorize the school building put up and furnished under the school law to be used for the purpose of teaching a Sunday school. If the precedent be established it may lead to great abuses and disagreeable altercations between different religious denominations which it is the purpose of the common school system to avoid." (67 Missouri, p. 301.)

Pennsylvania

In Hysong *vs.* Gallitzin Borough School District decided by the supreme court of Pennsylvania in 1894 one of the points was that "a school house having been erected for a particular corporate purpose the corporate authorities cannot authorize its use for any other, and any diversion is illegal and must be restrained when complained of." (164 Pennsylvania, p. 649.)

In Benden *vs.* Strabick the supreme court of Pennsylvania decided in 1897 that school directors have no authority to permit public school buildings to be used for sectarian religious meetings, for the holding of public lyceums, or for any other purposes other than school purposes directly relating to the instruction of the pupils of the schools, or for lectures or debates which are made a part of the course of instruction. If school buildings may be used for the convenience, pleasure, or instruction of the general public all other school property may be so used, and it is only a step further to apply funds to the same use. (182 Pennsylvania, p. 251.)

3. *What constitutes a sectarian school within the meaning of the Laws and the Constitutional provisions forbidding the appropriation of public money to such?*

Illinois

Under an act of 1879 entitled "An act to Aid Industrial Schools for Girls," etc., 189 female infants were brought before the county court of Cook County at various times between April 1, 1886, and June 4, 1887, on charges of being dependent girls. They were committed to the Industrial School for Girls at Chicago "to be in such school kept and maintained" until they arrived at the age of eighteen unless sooner discharged therefrom according to law. Suit was brought to recover for clothing and care, and tuition of said girls at the rate of $10.00 per month each. The Board of Commissioners of Cook County refused to pay the amounts asked, on the grounds that they were forbidden by the constitution to pay out any money in aid of sectarian schools.

It was charged by the County of Cook that the Chicago Industrial School for Girls never had any existence except on paper. It was a feeder for the "House of the Good Shepherd" and "St. Joseph's Orphan Asylum." All commitments nominally made to the former were in reality made to the latter two institutions. The former never furnished any clothing or rendered any service to these girls. The girls were really placed under the charge and care of the two latter institutions; they were taught, maintained and clothed by them alone. The House of the Good Shepherd was conducted by the Sisters of the Good Shepherd, a Roman Catholic order. St. Joseph's Orphan Asylum was conducted by the Sisters of Charity, a Roman Catholic order.

The supreme court of Illinois, in considering this case, known as the "County of Cook *vs.* The Chicago Industrial School for Girls," in 1888 decided as follows: "It follows from the foregoing statement of evidence that the House of the Good Shepherd and the St. Joseph Orphan Asylum are controlled by a church. Being such, they are necessarily sectarian in their character and in their objects. One of the definitions given by Webster of sectarianism is 'adherence to a separate religious denomination.'"

The only creed taught was the Catholic creed. Those who might not be instructed in the Catholic faith were not instructed in any faith. No provision was made for instruction in such creeds, other than the Catholic, as might be preferred by any of the inmates. " If the instruction is of a sectarian character the school is sectarian."

" The fact that an institution of learning teaches the doctrines of a particular church or sect, and that all exercises of a religious character are those of such church, will render the institution sectarian, within the meaning of Sec. 3, Art. 8, of the Constitution prohibiting payment from any public fund of anything in aid of any church or sectarian purpose, although all its pupils may not be instructed in such sectarian doctrines."

" The refusal to admit a judge of a court having the power to commit dependent girls to an industrial school into the place where such school is alleged to be kept, unless he should first obtain a permit from a bishop or member of the Roman Catholic church, is a strong circumstance tending to show that such school is controlled by that church."

" It cannot be said that a contribution is no aid to an institution because such contribution is made in return for services rendered or work done."

" If they are entitled to be paid out of the public funds even though they are under the control of sectarian denominations simply because they relieve the state of a burden which it would otherwise be itself required to bear, then there is nothing to prevent all public education from becoming subjected, by hasty and unwise legislation to sectarian influences. It is an untenable position that public funds may be paid out to help support sectarian schools provided only such schools shall render a *quid pro quo* for the payments made to them." (125 Illinois, p. 540.)

Maryland

In the case of St. Mary's Industrial School for Boys *vs.* George S. Brown, William G. Harrison and others; the Maryland Industrial School for Girls *vs.* Same; the St. Vincent's Infant Asylum of the City of Baltimore *vs.* Same; the Maryland Institute for the Promotion of the Mechanic Arts *vs.* Same; decided in 1876, the Maryland Court of Appeals held that the Mayor and City

Council of Baltimore had no authority to make appropriations, by the exercise of the taxing power to sustain or aid institutions, however benevolent and charitable in their character, which did not owe their creation to the municipal power conferred on the City of Baltimore, and were not created by the Legislature of the State, as instruments of municipal administration, but which were separate and distinct corporations, composed of private individuals and controlled by officers and agents of their own, and over which the city had no supervision or control, and for the management of which there was no accountability to the city whatever. Even though the State and city might be allowed to appoint representatives upon the boards of control of the first two of these institutions did not change the fact of their being private institutions, and as such ineligible to share in public funds. " The fact that the institutions may be under denominational or religious control, can in no manner affect their qualifiaction for assuming such relation to the city, or for the full and faithful discharge of the duties that they may contract to perform. Charity, to say the least of the matter, is quite as likely to be fully and faithfully administered under such auspices as it could be under any other. It could therefore be no objection that the institutions are or may be under the control and influence of those belonging to any particular church or denomination." (45 Maryland, p. 311.)

Massachusetts

In Jenkins *vs.* The Inhabitants of Andover, decided in 1869 by the supreme court of Massachusetts, it was held that a free school maintained as a charity under the direction of trustees elected by the town, who were to be members of certain religious societies, was not a public school entitled under the Massachusetts constitution to money raised by taxation for the support of public schools, which it provides shall never be appropriated to any religious sect for the maintenance exclusively of its own schools. (103 Massachusetts, p. 94.)

Mississippi

In 1879 the Mississippi Supreme Court had to pass upon the validity of the act quoted in part on page 47. The case was that of Charles H. Otken *vs.* J. S. Lamkin, County Superintendent, etc.

"An act of the Legislature passed March 5, 1878, entitled 'An Act to encourage the establishment of high schools and colleges in this State,' provides in effect, that whenever a child has attended a private institution of learning, which has secured a suitable building and a library of two hundred bound volumes of miscellaneous literature, and is conducted by a teacher or teachers of good moral and educational standing, such child, whether the school so attended by him be within or without the school district in which he resides, may receive from the common school fund the same *pro rata* share thereof to which he would have been entitled if he had attended the public free school of his district. The act contains no requirement that the private institutions therein contemplated shall be free from sectarian or religious control, nor that they shall be under the supervision of the State or county superintendent of public education, nor that they shall be free from the charge of tuition; but it does require that the pupils shall pay the tuition which may be exacted by the persons conducting the institutions; and, as it makes such institutions wholly private, the persons conducting them are permitted to exclude any pupils they may choose to reject. Held, that this act is in conflict with Article 8 of the State Constitution, and is therefore void." (56 Mississippi, p. 758.)

Nevada

In The State of Nevada *vs.* Hallock, decided by the supreme court of Nevada in 1882, it was held that the Nevada Orphan Asylum of Virginia City, Nevada, which was owned, controlled and presided over by a religious organization known as the Sisters of Charity, all of whom must be Catholics, and in which Catholic children were instructed in the doctrines of the Catholic church, while no special provision was made for giving religious instruction to Protestant children, was a sectarian institution and as such forbidden to draw any money from the state treasury by the constitutional provision forbidding the payment of any money from the state treasury for sectarian purposes. (16 Nevada, p. 373.)

New York

In The People *vs.* The Board of Education of Brooklyn, New York, the supreme court of that state decided in 1851 that the act of March 7, 1848, which declared that the orphan asylum societies of the City of Brooklyn should participate in the distribution of the school moneys raised in said city, in proportion to the number of children between the ages of four and sixteen years who had been under the charge of said societies and instructed in such manner as was usual in common schools, on the same basis as the common schools of said city, did not intend to bestow upon the asylum societies a share of the moneys arising from the revenues of the common school fund.

" If such were the design of the statute," says the court, " it would conflict with Art. 9, of the constitution, which provides that the capital of the common school fund shall be inviolate and that the revenue thereof shall be applied to the support of common schools."

The court held that the schools maintained by the Roman Catholic Orphan Asylum Society of the City of Brooklyn were not common schools within the meaning of the constitution.

" If the object of this special legislation is to afford them such education as the state furnishes to all it may as well and better be obtained through the ordinary channel. If the object is to furnish them with instruction of a partial or sectarian character, the state ought not and cannot constitutionally contribute to such a purpose."

The funds granted by the act in question were limited to those raised by the City of Brooklyn by tax upon its property. (13 *Barbour Supreme Court Reports,* p. 400.)

Likewise in St. Patrick's Orphan Asylum *vs.* The Board of Education of Rochester, New York, the supreme court decided in 1867 that money devoted by the constitution of the state for the support of common schools could not lawfully be appropriated to the support of incorporated orphan asylum societies, or for the support of common schools therein, as the latter are not common schools within the constitutional meaning of the term common school. (34 *Howard's Practice Reports,* p. 227.)

South Dakota

In The Synod of South Dakota *vs.* The State of South Dakota it was held by the supreme court of South Dakota in 1891 that the fact that the plaintiff corporation was organized and existed

to maintain and promulgate the doctrines and belief of the Chris-
tion religion known as Presbyterianism, and that it had offered
and given secular and sectarian instruction to divers and numerous students under its control, constituted it a sectarian school as
used in the constitution.

" Held that the law, in so far as it authorized the designation of
sectarian universities, colleges, or academies, by the territorial
board of education, in which classes should be instructed in
methods of teaching, was inconsistent with and repugnant to the
provisions of the state constitution and became inoperative and
ceased to be of binding force or effect after the adoption of the
state constitution within the state.

" Held that the prohibition in the constitution of any money or
other property to aid any sectarian school applied to all appropriations to such schools, whether made as a donation or in payment
for services rendered the state by such schools." (14 *Lawyers
Reports Annotated,* p. 418.)

Wisconsin

In The State *ex rel.* Weiss and Others *vs.* The District Board
of Edgerton, decided by the supreme court of Wisconsin in 1890,
it was held that the stated reading of the Bible in a public school
rendered it a religious seminary within the meaning of the Wisconsin constitution, Art. I, Par. 18, which prohibited the drawing
of money from the treasury for the benefit of religious
seminaries.

" The stated reading of the Bible as a text-book in the public
schools may be worship, and the school house thereby become, for
the time being, a place of worship, within the meaning of Sec. I,
Art. I, of the constitution, and to such use of the school house the
tax payers, who are compelled to aid in its erection and in the
maintenance of the school, have a legal right to object.

" Such reading being religious instruction, the money drawn
from the state treasury for the support of a school in which the
Bible is so read is for the benefit of a religious seminary within
the meaning of said section." (76 Wisconsin, p. 177.)

CONCLUSION

The foregoing citations from laws, from constitutional provisions, and from judicial decisions portray rather definitely some
of the more important phases of a process which has been going
on in this country for something over a hundred years, the
secularization of education.

The laws cited, which bear dates prior to 1776, and occasionally
one within the early national period, show as a rule the close
connection of church and school, of religion and education during
colonial days and the early years of the republic. They show the
largely religious aim of education, the largely religious nature of
the subject matter of instruction, and the considerable part played
by the church in the control of schools. They show the state
beginning to recognize the importance of education for her own
welfare and beginning to contribute to the support thereof, but
leaving unto the church a large measure of control in the supervision and administration of schools.

In the laws and constitutional provisions enacted subsequent to
about 1850, following an intervening period devoted largely to
local legislation, in which there is state legislation relating to
religion and education in but few states, we see the preponderance
of the church in educational affairs supplanted by that of the
state. The dominant aim of the school becomes a civic one, the
subject matter of instruction is purged of everything savoring of a
sectarian or denominational religious nature, and control shifts
from the church and her ministry to the state and her officials. Control of education becomes largely centralized, uniform series of
text-books and courses of study are provided for, provision is
made for state and county certification of teachers, and all forms
of religious tests for teachers or school officials are forbidden. Most
of the constitutional provisions have to do with safeguarding the
school revenues, derived from permanent funds and taxation,
against diversion to contending religious educational claimants,

and with protecting the schools themselves from the zeal of contending religious sects, who have sought from time to time to use
the public agencies of instruction for the propagation of their own
peculiar tenets.

In no less than thirty-five states has there been enacted specific
legislation or constitutional provisions against either sectarian
religious instruction or the use of text-books containing sectarian religious material, in state supported schools. While
usually the prohibition has been confined in the enactments to
" sectarian religion," yet practically this has come to mean all
religious instruction. The reading of the Holy Bible, which is
specifically provided for in the laws of at least fourteen states
and in the constitution of one, is practically the only remnant of
religious instruction now sanctioned by our state laws. Even
this is frequently limited by provisions specifying that those who
object to reading it or hearing it read shall be excused therefrom,
and the reading must be unaccompanied by any comments.

The question as to whether or not the reading of the Bible as a
part of the opening or closing exercises of the public schools constitutes sectarian religious instruction or the use of a sectarian
text-book has been passed upon in at least eleven of the twenty-
eight cases cited in Chapter XII. In all but three states in
which the supreme courts have passed upon this question, they
have held that it was not a sectarian book, and such use did not
constitute sectarian religious instruction within the meaning of
the legal or constitutional prohibitions. The exceptions are
Wisconsin, Nebraska, and Illinois. Usually the decisions
have been rendered, however, with the proviso that no comments
should be made thereon by the teacher, or that pupils who
objected should not be required to take part. I have found only
one case where reading from a specified version of the Bible was
held to be compulsory on all who attended school. This was in
Donahue *vs.* Richards, a Maine case decided in 1854. Frequently the courts have shifted the responsibility of determining
this question on the grounds that the selection of text-books was
a function of the local school board or that the reading of the
Bible in school was not in itself religious instruction of any kind.
In all the cases cited but one the issue has been raised by those
who objected to the Bible being read. The exception is that of

the Board of Education of the City of Cincinnati *vs.* Minor, in which objection was raised to the discontinuance of Bible reading in the schools.

There is a great mass of controversial literature bearing on this subject of religious instruction in the schools. Objection to and criticism of " Godless " public schools, etc., as well as articles, pamphlets, editorials, and books in defense of the secular school, but these lie outside the limits set for this study. State legislation, state constitutional provisions and state supreme court decisions seem best suited to give us the matured judgment of our people as a whole upon this subject.

At present there seem to be three fairly well defined attitudes according to which the American people can be classified in this connection: 1st. Those who are advocates of religious instruction in the public schools. Holding that character is more important than all else, and that religion is a necessary element in the process of forming right character, they would make religion one of the required subjects for all pupils. 2nd. Those who advocate religious, sectarian schools, in which sectarian doctrines may be freely taught by orthodox, denominational teachers. They claim that in educating the youth in such schools they are rendering to the state a distinct service, and are relieving the state of an obligation and a burden, and for this reason are entitled to state assistance. The state should be willing to reimburse them for the expense they are to in supplying schools and teachers. They will not be satisfied with non-sectarian religious instruction, but insist upon thorough indoctrination of the pupils in the doctrines of their particular church. 3rd. Those who have accepted the secular public school; who hold that it is no part of the duty of the state to teach religion; that under conditions such as exist in this country there is no other practicable course than the elimination of religious instruction from the public schools entirely, leaving it to the church, the Sunday-school, private enterprise, and the home to inculcate religious truth.

The secularization of public education represents but one phase of the differentiation and separation of the ecclesiastical and the civil powers which has been going on in this country from the earliest years of its history. The educational function has been especially dear unto the church and she has clung to it with the greatest tenacity, and in turn the church has had certain elements to contribute unto education which the people as a whole have been very loath to relinquish. But conditions have been such as seemingly to allow of no alternative to secularization, and to-day the principle of the secular school, however unwillingly and hesitatingly at first, has come to be accepted by a majority of our people in every state in the union. That some interpret this principle more liberally or more narrowly than others is true, but throughout the union such changes as have been made within recent years have been almost without exception in the direction of secularization. Some states have gone much farther with it than others. The older states have tended as a rule to abide most closely by the old practices and ideals. Some of the newer states of the West have taken the most advanced positions therein, others have lagged the farthest in the rear. Nowhere has there been a return to religious control, once the state has taken over the educational function. Nowhere has sectarian or denominational religious instruction been reinstated by any state after having been excluded. Nowhere has the work of education by the state for citizenship been acknowledged a failure and abandoned. Everywhere more and more of the revenues of the state are being devoted to educational ends. The American states have unbounded confidence in their ability to educate for their purposes.

BIBLIOGRAPHY

The following is a partial list of the sources cited or consulted in the course of this study.

PRIMARY SOURCES

Enactments of Colonial Legislative Powers.
Various forms of charters granted during the Colonial Period.
Session Laws of State and Territorial Legislatures.
State Codes and Revisals.
State School Laws.
State Constitutions.
The Federal and State Constitutions, Colonial Charters and other Organic Laws of the United States — Ben. Perley Poore.
State Supreme Court Reports.
Digests of Judicial Decisions.
Law Reporters.
Annual Reports of State Superintendents of Schools.
Governors' Messages.
Presidents' Messages.
The Annals of Education.
Annual Reports of City Superintendents of Schools.
Barnard's Journal.
Proceedings of the National Education Association.
The Catholic School System — Burns.
The Parochial School — Crowley.
The American Catholic Review.
Papers of the American Historical Association.
Charters, Acts and Official Documents Relating to Columbia University, Compiled by John B. Pine, New York, 1895.
The Niles Register.
Newspaper Files.
Educational and General Magazine Files.
Reports of the New York Public School Society.

SECONDARY SOURCES

History of Education in Alabama — Clark.
History of Education in Arkansas —Shinn.
History of the Public School System of California — Swett.

The History of Education in Connecticut — Steiner.
The History of Education in Delaware — Powell.
History of Education in Florida — Bush.
History of Education in Georgia — Jones.
Higher Education in Indiana — Woodburn.
Higher Education in Iowa — Parker.
History of Higher Education in Kentucky — Lewis.
The History of Education in Louisiana — Fay.
History of Higher Education in Maine — Hall.
History of Education in Maryland — Steiner.
History of Higher Education in Michigan — McLaughlin.
History of Education in Mississippi — Mayes.
Higher Education in Missouri — Snow.
History of Education in New Hampshire — Bush.
History of Education in New Jersey — Murray.
History of the Common School System of the State of New York—Randall.
History of Higher Education in the State of New York—Sherwood.
History of Education in North Carolina — Caldwell.
A History of Education in Pennsylvania — Wickersham.
History of Education in Rhode Island — Tolman.
History of Higher Education in South Carolina — Meriwether.
Higher Education in Tennessee — Merriam.
History of Education in Texas — Lane.
History of the Virginia Company of London — E. D. Neil.
Thomas Jefferson and the University of Virginia — Adams.
History of Education in West Virginia — Morgan and Clark.
The Evolution of the Massachusetts School System — Martin.
The Making of Our Middle Schools — Brown.
History of Education in the United States — Dexter.
Educational Legislation and Administration in the Colonies — Clews.
The Free School System — Adams.
Illustrative Educational Documents — Hinsdale.
Reports of the United States Commissioner of Education.
Federal Aid to Higher Education — Blackmar.
Economic Influences on Educational Advance — Carlton.
The Labor Movement in America — Ely.
Church and State in the United States — Schaff.
Columbia University Studies in Economics, History and Public Law,
    No. VI and No. XIII.
Johns Hopkins University Studies, Vol. XVII.
The Dutch and Quaker Colonies in America — Fiske
Atlantic Monthly, August, 1876.